S

AFRO-AMERICAN
RELIGIOUS MUSIC

AFRO-AMERICAN RELIGIOUS MUSIC

A Bibliography and A Catalogue of Gospel Music

Compiled by IRENE V. JACKSON

GREENWOOD PRESS
WESTPORT, CONNECTICUT • LONDON, ENGLAND

Library of Congress Cataloging in Publication Data

Jackson, Irene V
    Afro-American religious music.

    Includes indexes.
    1. Spirituals (Songs)--Bibliography. 2. Gospel
music--Bibliography. I. Title.
ML128.S4J3   016.7836'75   78-60527
ISBN 0-313-20560-4

Library of Congress Catalog Card Number: 78-60527
ISBN: 0-313-20560-4

First published in 1979

Greenwood Press, Inc.
51 Riverside Avenue, Westport, Connecticut 06880

Printed in the United States of America

10 9 8 7 6 5 4 3 2 1

To **ENRIQUE**

Contents

Preface

Scholarly interest in the Black religious music of Afro-Americans has been almost exclusively devoted to the study of one genre—the spiritual. The first collection of Afro-American spirituals was published in 1867, and scholarly investigation of this genre has continued full tilt to the present day. In musicological circles early research efforts centered on the origin of the spiritual—whether the first spiritual was black or white. This debate was prolonged until it was suggested and generally held, at least in musicological circles, that a give-and-take situation seemed likely.

The spiritual has been studied from a variety of perspectives. Accounts of this genre flourished beginning in the eighteenth century in the writings of missionaries, travelers, and others who were struck by this music. Yet most of these early writings suffered from erroneous conceptualization and interpretation. Apart from what is likely the first theological examination of the spiritual—Henry Hugh Proctor's thesis for the Yale Divinity School in the early part of the twentieth century—John Lovell's 1939 article, "The Social Implications of the Negro Spiritual," is generally regarded as the first serious attempt to explore the social meaning of the spiritual. Lovell's thesis was partially based on an idea introduced by Sterling Brown in *The Negro Poetry and Drama* (1937) that the social world of the slave is reflected in the spiritual. Prior to Lovell's article in 1939, significant contributions to the study of the spiritual were made by W. E. B. Du Bois in the chapter "The Sorrow Songs" from his book *Souls of Black Folk* (1903), Alain Locke in his book *The Negro and His Music* (1936), and James Weldon and J. Rosamund Johnson in their *Books of Negro Spirituals* (1925, 1926). Among white critics who made significant contributions to the study of the spiritual were Henry Krehbiel in *Afro-American Folksongs* (1914) and Howard Odum's and Guy B. Johnson's *The Negro and His Songs* (1925), and Milton Metfessel's *Phonophotography in Folk Music* (1928).

Despite the interest in the religious music of Afro-Americans there has been to date no general comprehensive history of the religious musical tradition of Blacks. The study that comes closest to examining the totality of religious music in the New World is John Lovell's *Black Song* (1972), yet little attention has been given to Black religious music in the Caribbean and South America. And also Lovell has left much unsaid about what this writer calls "the twentieth-century spiritual." The twentieth-century spiritual to which I refer is gospel music.

Gospel music has received the attention of scholars only within the last fifteen years. This attention, however, has been minimal—so much so that gospel music has been the most severely neglected area of twentieth-century Afro-American music, yet it is the most vital music celebrating the Black religious experience in the United States of this century. Gospel music, however, is an abundant storehouse from which other American musics have drawn mannerisms and technique.

The first scholarly study of gospel music appeared in 1960 as a dissertation by George Robinson Ricks. Since that time there have been less than ten dissertations or theses and only one book written on the subject.

This bibliography represents an attempt to demonstrate how an ethnomusicologist might examine gospel music within the context of New World Black religious music. As a research guide, this bibliography provides a conceptual framework on which the study of Black religious music of the New World can rest. Since literature on gospel music has not been readily accessible to the average investigator, this bibliography is intended to meet a basic research need.

In addition to articles researched by me, I have freely used bibliographies from books and articles. I have not included in this bibliography standard references except when germane to the scope of this bibliography. Although the bibliography is not nearly complete or exhaustive, it nonetheless constitutes a major effort toward the systematic organization of bibliographic materials that may form the basis for a comprehensive study of Afro-American religious music.

The conventional division of Afro-American religious music into three genres—spirituals, hymns, and gospels—is functionally useless because the terms are too often used in ways that do not correspond to basic historical or chronological matters. It is better if these terms are kept in the background momentarily and that attention be focused upon the processes that have given rise to Black religious musical traditions in the New World.

For the purpose of this bibliography Black and Afro-American religious music will include the music of established Black churches or denominations in the United States and the Caribbean as well as Afro-Christian cults in the Caribbean and South America. The bibliography also includes entries on West African music, particularly in the area of religious ritual. In this bibliography concern is focused on the impact of Christianity on traditional worship patterns.

That Black or Afro-American religious music of different geographical areas is included under the same rubric indicates that this music is a part of the same cultural matrix. For example, there are certain musical performance practices that persist in Black cults and churches whether they be in the Caribbean, the United States, or West Africa. Such practices as the use of percussion and percussive techniques, glossolalia, spirit possession, or dance are but a few examples of these persistent elements in Black religious ritual without geographical boundaries.

The first chapter, "Afro-America," includes general references to Afro-Americans in the United States. Pertinent anthropological and sociological studies have been included in this section. The second chapter includes references to ethnomusicology, dance, and folklore. "African and Afro-American Folksongs" constitutes the third chapter and includes general references that are significant to the Black religious music tradition. Chapter 4, "Religious Folksongs," includes entries on Afro-American spirituals, hymns, blues, and gospel. Standard references, whether books or articles, have been omitted from this chapter, particularly on the spiritual. Chapter 5, "Black Church/Black Religion," is limited primarily to the United States. The final chapter, "Caribbean," includes references about the religion, music, culture, folklore, and history of the West Indies, South America, and Bahamas.

Two indexes have been provided solely with the objective of facilitating use of the bibliography. Most entries have been cross-indexed. For articles that are out of print, the library where the entry was reviewed has been included; this was the case with Thomas A. Dorsey's *Dorsey's Songs with a Message,* which is located at the Schomburg Collection of the New York City Public Library.

The "Catalogue" lists the Library of Congress's holdings of Black gospels copyrighted between 1938 and 1965. Gospels are listed by composer or author, and each entry includes the name of the arranger, author, publishing company, and copyright year. This compilation reveals and documents several important points about the gospel tradition. For example, this compilation reveals that the major publishers and arrangers were often more significant than the actual composer. Also, a year-by-year analysis of gospel music activity could be reconstructed from the catalogue. The "Catalogue" is offered as an additional research tool and to stimulate further study of Afro-American gospel music.

Although this bibliography falls short of completeness or perfection, it will at least provide a basis for the study of Black religious music. Hopefully it will provoke further study and investigation.

Acknowledgments

This bibliography and catalogue are the result of a process that formally began
in 1969 when, as a senior at Howard University, I submitted a research paper on
Afro-American gospel music. Much of that research was based on the then unpublished notes of Pearl Williams-Jones, to whom I give credit for shaping my
budding intellectual "notions" regarding gospel music.

My research interest in gospel music continued in graduate school at Smith
College, where I was first introduced to the field of ethnomusicology by
Theodore Grame, who was a visiting faculty member at Smith College from
Wesleyan University and with whom I continued doctoral work at Wesleyan.
At Smith I was able to identify some few sources that dealt with gospel, but
the bibliography actually began to take shape as a result of a course in research
methods in ethnomusicology with Mark Slobin at Wesleyan. Jerome Long of
Wesleyan introduced the Black church and Black religion to me in a way that
was to broaden my conceptualization of gospel music. With David McAllester
I was made aware of anthropological tools and methods and began to understand how these tools are important in establishing a conceptual framework for
the study of gospel music in its social setting. During the summer of 1972 I did
fieldwork in Haiti and Jamaica. It was during this time that I came to realize
how an understanding of Afro-Christian cults and established churches of the
Caribbean are important to a study of gospel music.

During my dissertation year I was invited to join the Yale faculty, where I
introduced a course entitled "Black Sacred Music in the United States." William
Waite of the music department and Charles Davis of the Afro-American studies
department were generous in their support of this new course. Through this
course I was able to continue expanding the bibliography. Through a Griswold
Research Grant from Yale University that I received in 1975, I was able to
further explore the ethnomusicology of religious cults and churches in Jamaica

xivACKNOWLEDGMENTS

and was thus able to unearth literature in this area. From my association with my former Yale colleagues—William Ferris in folklore, Al Raboteau and James Washington in religious studies, and Robert Thompson in art history—I was better able to focus and refine the scope of the bibliography.

A special thanks is extended to all the Yale students who took the course over the years and especially to the students whose insightful remarks, questions, and comments guided me and helped me rethink the actual presentation of the course. Students who readily come to mind in this regard are Suzanne Spellen, who as my undergraduate assistant was active in my bibliographic search, Leslie Downey, whose comments in class always made me think, and Derrick Bochannan, who wrote to me years after taking the course to say that the course was a significant experience in his life.

To Gwendolyn Williams, I owe a lot for the typing of the first draft of this work. To Enrique and Guillermo, who endured as I searched for sources, a big kiss. And to my parents, thanks.

Illustrations

Bibliography

1

Afro-America: General History, Culture, Anthropology, and Sociology

1. Abrahams, Roger D. "Negro Stereotypes," Journal of American Folklore, 83 (1970) 229-235.

2. Aptheker, Herbert, ed. A Documentary History of the Negro People, Vols I, II. New York: Citadel Press, 1951.

3. Baker, Ross K., ed. Afro-American Readings. Florence, Kentucky: Van Nos Reinhold, 1970.

4. Baskin, Wade and Richard N. Runes. Dictionary of Black Culture. New York: Philosophical Library, 1973.

5. Bastide, Roger. African Civilizations in the New World. New York: Harper and Row, 1971.

6. Bender, Eugene I and George Kagiwada. "Hansen's Law of Third-Generation Return and the Study of American Religio-Ethnic Groups," Phylon, 29 (Winter 1968) 360-370.

7. Beynon, Erdmann Doane. "The Voodoo Cult Among Negro Migrants in Detroit," American Journal of Sociology, 43 (1938) 894-907.

8. Blassingame, John W. The Slave Community. New York: Oxford University Press, 1973.

9. Bontemps, Arna and Langston Hughes. The Book of Negro Folklore. New York: Dodd-Meade, 1958.

10. Botkin, B.A. Lay My Burden Down. Chicago: University Press, 1945.

11. Brawley, Benjamin. "The Negro Genius," Southern Workman, 44 (1915) 305-308.

12. _____. Negro Genius; a New Approach. 1937
reprint edition, New York: Appollo Eds, 1970.

13. _____. A Social History of the American Negro.
New York: Macmillan, 1970.

14. Brewer, J. Mason, ed. American Negro Folklore. New York:
Quadrangle, 1974.

15. Butcher, Margaret J. The Negro in American Culture. 2nd
edition, New York: Knopf, 1972.

16. Chicago Commission on Race Relations, eds. Negro in
Chicago: A Study of Race Relations and a Race Riot. 1922
reprint, New York: Arno Press, 1968.

17. Clark, Kenneth B. Dark Ghetto. New York: Harper-Row, 1965.

18. Courlander, Harold. A Treasury of Afro-American Folklore.
New York: Crown Publishers, Inc., 1976.

19. Crowley, Daniel J., ed. African Folklore in the New World.
Austin: University of Texas Press, 1977.

20. Culin, S. "Negro Sorcery in the U.S.," Journal of American Folklore, 3 (1890) 281-287.

21. "The Debate Over Race: A Study in the Sociology of
Knowledge," Phylon, 29 (1968) 127-141.

22. Dollard, John. Caste and Class in a Southern Town. New
Haven: Yale University Press, 1937.

23. Dorson, Richard M. American Negro Folktales. New York:
Fawcett World, 1974.

24. Dowd, Jerome. The Negro in American Life. New York:
Century Publishing Co., 1926.

25. Dundes, Alan, ed. Mother Wit from the Laughing Barrel.
Readings in the Interpretation of Afro-American Folklore.
Englewood Cliffs: Prentice-Hall, Inc., 1973.

26. Fishwick, M. "Black Popular Culture," Journal Popular
Culture, 4 (1971) 637-645.

27. Franklin, John Hope. From Slavery to Freedom: A History
of American Negroes. 4 ed, New York: Knopf, 1974.

28. Frazier, E. Franklin. "The Occupational Differentiation
of the Negro in Cities," Southern Workman. 59 (1930) 195a-
200a.

29. Gayle, Jr. Addison, ed. The Black Aesthetic. Garden City,
N.Y.: Doubleday and Co., Inc., 1971.

30. Goldstein, Rhoda L., ed. Black Life and Culture in the
United States. New York: Thomas Y. Crowell Co., 1971.

31. Hannery, ULF. Soulside: Inquiries into Ghetto Culture
and Community. New York: Columbia University Press, 1969.

32. Harris, Middleton. The Black Book. New York: Random House,
1974.

33. Haskins, James. Witchcraft, Mysticism and Magic in the
Black World. Garden City, N.Y.: Doubleday, 1974.

34. Hershovits, Melville J. The American Negro. N.Y.: A.A.
Knopf, 1928.

35. _____. "Freudian Mechanisnes in Primitive
Negro Psychology," In E.E. Evans-Pritchard et al (eds)
Essays Presented to C.G. Seligman. London: Kegan Paul, Trench,
Trubner, 1934, 75-84.

36. _____. "Social History of the Negro," A Handbook of Social Psychology. ed. Carl Murchison. Worchester,
Mass.: Clark University Press, 1935. 38-64.

37. _____. "The Interdisciplinary Aspects of
Negro Studies," Washington, D.C.: American Council of
Learned Societies, 1941.

38. _____. Patterns of Negro Music. Music Division,
Library of Congress, 194__.

39. _____. "Some Next Steps in the Study of Negro,"
Journal of American Folklore, 56 (1943) 1-17.

40. _____. Acculturation: the Study of Culture
Contact. Gloucester, Mass.: P. Smith, 1958.

41. _____. The Myth of the Negro Past. Boston:
Beacon Press, 1958.

42. _____. The New World Negro. Bloomington:
Indiana University Press, 1966.

43. Hooks, Rosie L. Black People and Their Culture: Selected
Writings from the African Diaspora. Washington, D.C.:
Smithsonian, 1978.

44. Hughes, Langston and Arna Bontemps, ed. Book of Negro
Folklore. New York: Dodd, Mead and Co., 1958.

45. Hughes, Langston, Milton Meltzer and C. Eric Lincoln.
A Pictorial History of Blackamericans. 4th ed. New York:
Crown Publishers, 1967.

46. Hyatt, Harry M. Hoodoo, Conjuration, Witchcraft and Rootwork. Hannibal, Mo.: Western Pub., 1970.

47. Jackson, Bruce. The Negro and His Folklore in Nineteenth Century Periodicals. Austin: University of Texas Press, 1967.

48. Jackson, Bruce. Get Your Ass in the Water and Swim Like Me!: Narrative Poetry From Black Oral Tradition. Cambridge: Harvard University Press, 1974.

49. Jaffe, Harry Joe. "American Negro Folklore: A Checklist of Scarce Items," Southern Folklore Quarterly, 36 (1972) 68-70.

50. Johnson, Charles S. Shadow of the Plantation. Chicago: University of Chicago Press, 1934.

51. Johnson, James Weldon. Black Manhattan. New York: A. A. Knopf, 1930.

52. Johnson, James Weldon. "Contributions of the Negro to American Culture," Southern Workman, 67 (1938) 57-60.

53. Karon, Bertram P. The Negro Personality. New York: Springer Publishing Co., 1955.

54. Kochman, Thomas, ed. Rappin' and Stylin' Out Communication in Urban Black America. Urbana: University of Illinois Press, 1972.

55. Leeds, Morton. "The Process of Cultural Stripping and Reintegration (the Rural Migrant in the City)," Journal of American Folklore, 83 (1970) 259-268.

56. Levine, Lawrence W. Black Culture and Black Consciousness. New York: Oxford University Press, 1977.

57. McKay, Claude. Harlem: Negro Metropolis. New York: E. P. Dutton and Co., 1940.

58. Meier, August and Elliott M. Rudwich. From Plantation to Ghetto. New York: Hill and Wang, 1966.

59. Puckett, Newbill N. Folk Beliefs of the Southern Negro. New York: Dover Publications, 1926.

60. Schatz, Walter. Directory of Afro-American Resources. Ann Arbor: Bowker, 1970.

61. Smith, Arthur L., ed. Language, Communication, and Rhetoric in Black America. New York: Harper and Row, 1972.

62. Spalding, Henry D. Encyclopedia of Black Folklore and Humor. Middle Village, N.Y.: Jonathan David Publishers, 1972.

63. Spear, Allan H. Black Chicago the Making of a Negro Ghetto 1890-1920. Chicago: The University of Chicago Press, 1967.

64. Szwed, John F., ed. Black America. New York: Basic Books, 1970.

65. Szwed, John F. and Roger D. Abrahams. Afro-American Folk Culture: An Annotated Bibliography of Materials from North, Central and South America and the West Indies, 2 volumes. New York: Institute for the Study of the Humanities, 1977.

66. Whitten, Norman E. and John F. Szwed. Afro-American Anthropology. New York: The Free Press, 1970.

67. Work, Monroe. "Some Parallelisms in the Development of Africans and other Races," Southern Workman, V 35 (1906) 614-621, 166-175; V 36 (1907) 36-43, 105-111.

2

Ethnomusicology, Dance, and Folklore

68. Arvey, Verna. "Negro Dance and its Influence on Negro Music," in Black Music in Our Culture. Dominique-Rene de Lerma, ed., Kent, Ohio: The Kent State University Press, 1970, 79-92.

69. Berofsky, Barbara. "Kinesiology as an Aid in the Recording of Dances," Ethnomusicology, XI (1967) 234-237.

70. Blacking, John. "How Musical is Man? Seattle: University of Washington Press, 1973.

71. Bright, William. "Language in Music: Areas for Cooperation," Ethnomusicology, (1963) 26-32.

72. Brunvand, Jan Harold. The Study of American Folklore. New York: W.W. Norton and Co., Inc., 1968.

73. Chase, Gilbert. "A Dialectical Approach to Music History." Ethnomusicology, 2 (1958) 1-9.

74. _____. America's Music, rev. edition. New York: McGraw-Hill Book Company, 1966.

75. _____. "American Musicology and Social Sciences," Perspectives in Musicology, Barry Brook, comp. New York: W.W. Norton, 1972, 85-103.

76. Chilkovsky, Nadia. "Analysis and Notation of Basic Afro-American Movements," in Jazz Dance, Marshall and Jean Stearns, eds, New York: Macmillan, 1968, 421-449.

77. Clark, Edgar Rogie. "Folk Music Confusion," The Music Journal, VII (1949) 10, 32-33.

78. Coffin, Tristram Porter, ed. Our Living Traditions. New York: Basic Books, 1968.

79. Crowley, Daniel J. "Aesthetic Judgment and Cultural Relativism," Journal of Aesthetics and Art Criticism 17 (1958) 187-193.

80. De Jager, Hugo. "Music Regarded from a Sociological Point of View," Music and Man, 1 (1974) 162-167.

81. Del Perugia, Paul "From Music to Ecstasy." Journal World Music, XIII/3 (1971) 3-17.

82. Diserens, Charles, M. The Influence of Music in Behavior. Princeton: Princeton University Press, 1926.

83. Dorson, Richard. "Is There a Folk in the City? Journal of American Folklore 83 (1970) 185-191.

84. _____. Folklore and Folklife. Chicago: University of Chicago Press, 1972.

85. Draper, David Elliott. "The Mardi Gras Indians: The Ethnomusicology of Black Associations in New Orleans." Ph.D. dissertation, 1973, Tulane University.

86. Dundes, Alan. The Study of Folklore. Englewood Cliffs, N.J.: Prentice-Hall, 1965.

87. Emery, Lynn Fauley. Black Dance in the United States from 1619 to 1970. Palo Alto: National Press Books, 1972.

88. Essays for a Humanist: An Offering to Klaus Wachsman. Spring Valley, N.Y.: Town House Press, 1977.

89. Etykorn, Peter K. "Social Context of Songwriting in the United States," Ethnomusicology 7 (1963) 96-106.

90. Evans, David. "Afro-American Folklore," Journal of American Folklore 86 (1973) 413-434.

91. Freeman, Linton C., Allen P. Merriam. "Statistical Classification in Anthropology: an Application to Ethno-musicology," American Anthropologist 58 (1956) 464-472.

92. Freeman, Linton C. "The Changing Functions of a Folksong," Journal of American Folklore. 70 (1957) 215-220.

93. Glass, Paul. "A Hiatus in American Music History," The Black Prism: Perspectives on the Black Experience, Inez Smith Reid, ed. New York: C.U.N.Y., Faculty Press, 1969, 35-48.

94. Goines, Margaretta Bobo. "African Retentions in the Dance of the Americas," Dance Research Monograph One, 1971-72, New York: Cord, 1973, 209-229.

95. Goldstein, Kenneth S. A Guide for Field Workers in Folk-lore. Platboro, Penn.: Folklore Associates, Inc., 1964.

96. Grame, Theodore C. "Ethnic Music," Carnegie Magazine (Pittsburgh), 49 (March 1975) 109-114.

97. Greenway, John. Ethnomusicology. Boulder: University of Colorado, 1976.

98. Gustafson, R. "Folk Music and Social Protest," Liberation. 7 (1962) 26-34.

99. Hamm, Charles and Bruno Nettle and Ronald Byrnside. Contemporary Music and Music Cultures. Englewood Cliffs, New Jersey: Prentice-Hall, Inc., 1975.

100. Ham, Shirley. "The Problems Encountered by Missionaries in Adapting Christian Hymnody to Non-Western Cultures," M.A. thesis, 1954, Columbia Bible College, South Carolina.

101. Hanna, Judith Lynn. "Africa's New Traditional Dances," Ethnomusicology. 9 (1965) 13-21.

102. _____. "Field Research in African Dances: Opportunities and Utilities," Ethnomusicology 12 (1968) 101-106.

103. Hansen, Chadwick. "Jenny's Toe: Negro Shaking Dances in America," American Quarterly 19 (1967) 554-63.

104. Harap, Louis. Social Roots of the Arts. New York: International Publishers, 1949.

105. Harrison, Frank. "Music and Culture: the Function of Music in Social and Religious Systems," Perspectives in Musicology. Barry S. Brook, ed. New York: Norton, 1972, 133-151.

106. Hayworth, C. Bibliography of North American Folklore and Folksong. 2nd ed., New York: Dover Publication, 1961.

107. Herskovits, Melville J. "Patterns of Negro Music," Transactions Illinois State Academy of Sciences 34 (September 1941) 19-23.

108. _____. "The Hypothetical Situation: A Technique of Field Research," Southwestern Journal of Anthropology 6 (1950) 32-40.

109. Herzog, George "The Study of Folksong in America," Southern Folklore Quarterly 2 (1938) 59-64.

110. Hitckcock, H. Wiley. "Americans in American Music," College Music Symposium VIII (Fall 1968) 131-142.

111. Hood, Mantle. "Training and Research Methods in Ethnomusicology," Ethnomusicology Newsletter, No. 11 (1957) 2-8.

112. _____ . The Ethnomusicologist. L.A.: University of California Press, 1971.

113. Jackson, Glorianne and Margaret Thompson Drewal. Sources on African and African Related Dance. New York: American Dance Guild, 1974.

114. Karpeles, Maud, ed. The Collecting of Folk Music and Other Ethnomusicological Material: a Manual for Field Workers: London: International Folk Music Council, 1958.

115. Kealiinohomioku, Joann Wheeler. "A Comparative Study of Dance as a Constellation of Motor Behaviors Among African and United States Negroes," M.A. thesis, Northwestern University, 1965.

116. Kinney, Esi Sylvia. "Africanisms in Music and Dance of the Americas," Rhoda L. Goldstein, ed., Black Life and Culture in the United States. New York: Thomas Y. Crowell Co., 1971.

117. Kolinski, Mieczyslaw. "Classification of Tonal Structures Illustrated by a Comparative Chart of American Indian, Afro-American, and English-American Structures," Studies in Ethnomusicology 1 (1961) 38-76.

118. Kunst, Jaap. Some Sociological Aspects of Music. Washington: The Library of Congress, 1958.

119. _____ . Ethnomusicology: A Study of its Nature, its Problems, Methods and Representative Personalities to Which is Added a Bibliography. The Hague: Martinus Nijhoff, 1974.

120. Kurath, Gertrude. "Stylistic Blends in Afro-American Dance Cults of Catholic Origin," (Papers of the Michigan Academy of Science, Arts and Letters) 48 (1963) 577-81.

121. _____ . "African Influences on American Dance," Focus on Dance 3 (1965) 34-50.

122. Lange, Roderyk. The Nature of Dance: An Anthropological Perspective. London: MacDonald and Evans, 1975.

123. _____ . "Some Notes on the Anthropology of Dance," Dance Studies (Les Bois, St. Peter, Jersey, C.I., U.K.) (1976) 38-46.

124. Lekis, Lisa. Dancing Gods. Metuchen, New Jersey: Scarecrow Press, 1960.

125. Lomax, Alan. "Folk Song Style," American Anthropologist 61 (1959) 927-954.

126. _____. Folk Song Style and Culture. Washington:
American Association for the Advancement of Science, 1968.

127. McAllester, David P. Readings in Ethnomusicology. New
York: Johnson Reprint Corporation, 1971.

128. McCue, George, ed., Music in American Society. New Brunswick, New Jersey: Transaction Books, 1976.

129. McLeod, Norma. "Ethnomusicological Research and Anthropology," Annual Review of Anthropology 3 (1974) 99-115.

130. Meerloa, Joost A.M. Dance Craze and Sacred Dance. London:
Peter Owen, 1962.

131. Meyer, Leonard. "Universalism and Relativsm in the Study
of Ethnic Music," Ethnomusicology 4 (1960) 49-54.

132. Merriam, Alan P. "The Use of Music in the Study of a
Problem of Acculturation," American Anthropoligist 57 (1955)
28-34.

133. _____. "Ethnomusicology: Discussion and Definition of the Field," Ethnomusicology 4 (1960) 107-114.

134. _____. The Anthropology of Music. Evanston:
Northwestern University Press, 1964.

135. Metfessel, Milton F. Phonophotography in Folk Music.
Chapel Hill: University of North Carolina, 1928.

136. Neher, Andrew. "A Physiological Explanation of Unusual
Behavior in Ceremonies Involving Drums," Human Biology
34 (1962) 151-160.

137. Nettl, Bruno. "Some Linguistic Approaches to Music
Analysis," Journal International Folk Music Council 10 (1958)
36-41.

138. _____. Music in Primitive Culture. Cambridge:
Harvard University Press, 1956.

139. _____. "Historical Aspects of Ethnomusicology,"
American Anthropologist 60 (1958) 518-532.

140. _____. Theory and Method in Ethnomusicology.
New York: The Free Press, 1964.

141. _____. "Comparison and Comparitive Method in
Ethnomusicology," Yearbook of the International-American
Musical Research, IX (1973) 148-161.

142. _____. Folk Music in the United States an
Introduction. Detroit: Wayne State University Press, 1976.

143. Nketia, K.H. "Possession Dances in African Societies," International Folk Music Council Bulletin 9 (1957) 4-9.

144. Parker, William R. "The Relationship Between the Humanities and the Social Sciences: Report of Discussion," American Council of Learned Societies Newsletter 12 (March, 1961) 14-18.

145. Primus, Pearl. "Black America-Dance of the Spirit," Focus on Dance 6 (1972) 20-22.

146. Ramey, Michael James. "A Classification of Musical Instruments for Comparative Study," Ph.D. dissertation U.C.L.A., 1974.

147. Rhodes, Willard. "Music as an Agent of Political Expression," Sing-Out! XIII (1963) 32-41.

148. Sachs, Curt. The Wellsprings of Music. The Hague: Martinus Nijhoff, 1962.

149. Silberman, Alphons. The Sociology of Music. London: Routledge & Kegan Paul, 1963.

150. Wachsmann, Klaus P. Essays on Music and History in Africa. Evanston: Northwestern University Press, 1971.

151. Warren, Lee. The Dance of Africa. Englewood Cliffs, N.J.: Prentice-Hall, 1972.

152. Willener, Alfred. "Music and Sociology," Cultures, Music and Society. I (1971) 233-249.

3

African and Afro-American Folksongs

153. "African Influences and the Blues: an Interview With Richard A. Waterman," Living Blues 2 (1971) 30-36.

154. "African Native Music," Southern Workman 55 (1926) 396-397.

155. Allen, W.F., C.P. Ware and L.M. Garrison. Slave Songs of the United States. New York: A. Simpson and Co., 1867.

156. Ames, Russell. "Protest and Irony in Negro Folksong," Science and Society XIV (1950) n.p.

157. _____. "Implications of Negro Folk Song," Science and Society. XVI (1951) n.p.

158. Anderson, Hilton. "Some Negro Slave Songs From an 1856 Novel," Mississippi Folklore Register 8 (1974) 221-226.

159. Appleton, C.R. "The Comparative Preferential Response of Black and White College Students to Black and White Folk and Popular Musical Styles," Ph.D. dissertation, 1970, N.Y.U.

160. "Art in Music," Crisis I (1928) 22-31.

161. Arvey, Verna. "Afro-American Music Memo," Music Journal 27 (1969) 36, 68-69.

162. Baker, David N. "A Periodization of Black Music History," Reflections on Afro-American Music. Dominque Rene de Lerma, ed., Kent: The Kent State University Press, 1973, 143-160.

163. "Balk At Folk Songs: Howard University Students Threaten to Revolt," Washington Post. Dec. 19, 1909, n.p.; Dec. 20, 1909 n.p.; Dec. 21, 1909, n.p.

164. Barrett, Harris. "Negro Folksongs," Southern Workman
41 (1912) 238-245.

165. Bartholomew, Marshall. "Your Own Music," Southern Workman
56 (1927) 398.

166. Bass, R. D. "Negro Songs from the Pedree County (South
Carolina)," Journal of American Folklore 44 (1931) 418.

167. Bastin, Bruce. "The Devil's Goin' to Get You," North
Carolina Folklore Journal 21 (1973) 189-194.

168. Bebey, Francis. African Music, A People's Art. New York:
Lawrence Hill & Co., 1975.

169. Belz, Carl I. "Popular Music and the Folk Tradition,"
Journal of American Folklore 80 (1967) 130-135.

170. "Bibliography of Negro Folksongs," Journal of American
Folklore 24 (1911) 393-394.

171. "Black Music and Its Future Transmutation into Real Art,"
Current Opinion 63 (1917) 27-37.

172. Bluestein, Eugene. "The Background and Sources of an
American Folksong Tradition," Ph.D. dissertation, 1960,
University of Minnesota.

173. Brooks, Tilford. "The Black Musician in American Society,"
Music Journal 33 (1975) 40-45.

174. Brown, John Mason. "Songs of the Slave," Lippencott's
Magazine 2 (1868) 617-619.

175. Browne, Ray B. "Some Notes on the Southern 'Holler,'"
Journal of American Folklore 67 (1954) 73-77.

176. Bruce, J.E. "A History of Negro Musicians," Southern
Workman 10 (1916) 569-573.

177. Burlin, Natalie Curtis. "How Negro Folk-Songs are 'Born,'"
Current Opinion 66 (1919) 165-166.

178. _____. "Recognition of Negro Music," Southern
Workman 49 (1920) 6-7.

179. Byrd, Donald. "The Meaning of Black Music," Black
Scholar 3 (1972) 28-31.

180. Carlisle, N.T. "Old Time Darkey Plantation Melodies,"
Texas Folklore Society Publication 5 (1926) 137-143.

181. Clark, Edgar Rogie. Moment Musical: Ten Selected News-
paper Articles by E.R. Clark. Fort Valley, Ga.: Dept. of
Music, Fort Valley State College, 1940.

182. _____. "Negro Folk Music in America," Journal of American Folklore 64 (1951) 281-290.

183. Courlander, Harold. Negro Folk Music U.S.A. New York: Columbia University Press, 1963.

184. Crawford, Portia Naomi. "A Study of Negro Folk Songs from Greensboro, North Carolina and Surrounding Towns," North Carolina Forklore Register 16 (1968) 65-139.

185. Cray, Ed. "An Acculturative Continuum for Negro Folk Song in the United States," Ethnomusicology 5 (1961) 10-15.

186. Curtis, Natalie Burlin. "Black Singers and Players," The Musical Quarterly 5 (1919) 499-504.

187. _____. "Negro Music at Birth," The Musical Quarterly 5 (1919) 86-89.

188. Dane, Barbara. "Black Music Today," Guardian (May 25, 1968) 34.

189. de Lerma, Dominque-Reni. Black Music in College and University Curricula. Kent State University Press, Kent, Ohio: 1970.

190. _____. Black Music Now: A Source Book on 20th Century Black American Music. Kent, Ohio: Kent State University Press, 1970.

191. _____. "Dett and Engel," The Black Perspective in Music (Spring, 1973) 70-72.

192. _____. Reflections on Afro-American Music. Kent, Ohio: Kent State University Press, 1973.

193. Dett, Nathaniel "The Emancipation of Negro Music," Southern Workman 47 (1918) 176-186.

194. _____. "Ethnologist Aids Composer to Draw Inspiration from Heart of People," Musical America 30 (1919) n.p.

195. _____. "Folk Song of the American Negro," Southern Workman 45 (1916) 125-126.

196. Engel, Carl. An Introduction to Study of National Music. New York: AMS Press, 1976.

197. Epstein, Dana. "Slave Music in the U.S. Before 1860: A Survey of Sources," Notes (Summer 1963) 377-390.

198. _____. "The Search for Black Music's African Roots," University of Chicago Magazine 66 (1973) 18-22.

199. Fisher, Miles Mark. Negro Slave Songs of the United States. New York: Citadel Press, 1969.

200. "The Folksong Revival: A Symposium," New York Folklore Quarterly 19 (1963) 83-142.

201. Garrett, Romeo B. "African Survivals in American Culture," Journal of Negro History 51 (1966) 239-245.

202. "The Gateway of Music," Southern Workman 57 (1928) 108-109.

203. Gehikens, K.A. "Negro in Various Fields of Music," Etude 53 (1935) 375.

204. George, Zelma. "A Bibliographical Index to Negro Music," Moreland-Springarn Collection, Howard University.

205. _____. "Negro Music in American Life," John Davis, ed. American Negro Reference Book John Davis, ed. New York: Prentice Hall, 1966, 731-758.

206. Goines, Leonard. "Walk Over'. "Music in the Slave Narratives," Sing-Out! ' 24 (1976) 6-11.

207. Griffin, George H. "Slave Music of the South," American Missionary 36 (1882) 70-72.

208. Hallowell, Emily, ed. Calhoun Plantation Songs. Boston: C.W. Thompon & Co. 1901.

209. Haralambos, Michael. "Soul Music and Blues: Their Meaning and Relevance in Northern United States Black Ghettos," in Norman Whitten and John Szwed, eds. Afro-American Anthropology. New York: The Free Press, 267-284.

210. Harris, Barrett. "Negro Folksong," Southern Workman 41 (1912) 238-245.

211. Hare, Maude Cuney. "The Drum in Africa: Use of Music by Primitive People," Musical Observer (July, 1918) n.p.

212. _____. Negro Musicians and Their Music. Washington, D.C.: Associate Publishers, 1936.

213. Heckman, Don. "Black Music and White America," Black America. John Szwed, ed. New York: Basic Books, 1970, 158-170.

214. Herskovits, Melville J. "Patterns of Negro Music," Transactions 34 (1941) 19-23.

215. Hickerson, Joseph C. "A List of Folklore and Folk Music Archives and Related Collections in the U.S. and Canada," Washington, D.C.: Library of Congress, 1975.

216. Hornbostel, E.M. "American Negro Songs," International Review of Missions 15 (1926) 750.

217. Howard, Joseph H. Drums in the Americas. New York: Oak, 1967.

218. Howard, John Tasker, Jr. "Capturing the Spirit of the Real Negro Music; First Accurate Recordings by Natalie Curtis Burlin of Negro Part singing," The Musician 24 (1919) 13-41.

219. Howe, R. Wilson. "The Negro and His Songs," Southern Workman 51 (1922) 381-383.

220. Jackson, Clyde Owen. The Songs of our Years; A Study of Negro Folk Music. New York: Exposition Press, 1968.

221. Jackson, Eileen S., "The Use of Negro Folksong in Symphonic Forms," M.A. thesis, 1941, University of Chicago.

222. Jackson, Richard. United States Music; a Source of Bibliography and Collective Bibliography. Brooklyn: Institute for Studies in American Music, 1973.

223. Jefferson, Margo. "Ripping off Black Music: from Thomas 'Daddy' Rice to Jimi Hendrix," Harper's 245 (1973) 40-45.

224. Jenkins, Mildred Leona. "The Impact of African Music upon the Western Hemisphere," M.A. thesis, 1942, Boston University.

225. Jessup, Lynn Elva. "African Characteristics Found in Afro-American and Anglo-American Music," M.A. thesis, 1971, University of Washington.

226. Johnson, Guy B. The Quality of Negro Voices. Chapel Hill, North Carolina: University of North Carolina Press, 1928.

227. _____. "The Negro and Musical Talent," Southern Workman 56 (1927) 439-444.

228. Jones, A.M. African Music. Livingstone, Northern Rhodesia: The Rhodes-Livingston Museum, 1949.

229. Jones, Leroy. Blues People. New York: William Morrow and Co., 1963.

230. Jones, Solomon and Paul Tanner. "Afro-American Music: Black Moans," Music Journal 28 (1970) 36-37.

231. Katz, Bernard. The Social Implications of Early Negro Music in the United States. New York: Arno Press, 1969.

232. Keil, Charles. Urban Blues. Chicago University of Chicago Press, 1966.

233. Kennedy, Robert. Mellows; a Chronicle of Unknown Singers.
New York: A and C Boni, 1925.

234. Kenscella, Hazel Gertrude. "Songs of the American Negro
and Their Influence upon Composed Music," M.A. thesis, 1934,
Columbia University.

235. Kirby, Percival R. "A Study of Negro Harmony," Musical
Quarterly 16 (1930) 404-414.

236. Kmen, Henry A. "Old Corn Meal: A Forgotten Urban Negro
Folksinger," Journal of American Folklore 75 (1962) 29-34.

237. Krehbiel, Henry. Afro-American Folksongs. New York:
Frederick Ungar Publishing Co., 1962.

238. Ladner, Robert Jr. "Folk Music, Pholk Music and the
Angry Children of Malcolm X," Southern Folklore Quarterly
34 (1970) 131-145.

239. Landeck, Beatrice. Echoes of Africa in Folk Songs of
the Americas. New York: McKay, 1961.

240. Laubenstein, Paul Fritz. "Race Values in Aframerican
Music," Musical Quarterly 16 (1930) 131-146.

241. "Legitimizing the Music of the Negro," Current Opinion
54 (1913) 384-385.

242. Levine, Lawrence W. Black Culture and Black Consciousness:
Afro-American Folk Thought From Slavery to Freedom. New York:
Oxford University Press, 1977.

243. _____. "Slave Songs and Slave Consciousness,"
An Exploration in Nineteenth Century Social History, Tamara
Hareven, ed. Englewood-Cliffs; Prentice-Hall, 1971, 99-130.

244. Locke, Alain. "Negro Folk Songs," Southern Workman   54
(1925) 533.

245. _____. The Negro and His Music/Negro Art: Past
and Present. New York: Arno Press, 1969.

246. _____. "Toward a Critique of Negro Music,"
Opportunity 12 (1934) 328-331, 365-367.

247. Lomax, Alan. "Africanisms in New World Music," in
Papers of the Conference on Research and Resources of Haiti,
Research Institute on the Study of Man. New York: Columbia
University, 1969.

248. _____. "The Homogeneity of African and Afro-
American Musical Style," Afro-American Anthropology Norman
Whitten and John Szwed, eds. New York: The Free Press, 1970,
181-202.

249. Longini, Murriel Davis. "Folksongs of Chicago Negroes," Journal of American Folklore 52 (1939) 96-11.

250. Lornell, Christopher. "Pre-blues Black Music in Piedmont North Carolina," North Carolina Folklore Journal 23 (1975) 26-32.

251. Lucas, John Samuel. "Rhythms of Negro Music and Negro Poetry," M.A. thesis 1945, University of Minnesota.

252. Margetson, Edward. "Folk Music," 56 (1927) Southern Workman. 487-492.

253. McAdams, Nettie I. "The Folksongs of the American Negro; a Collection of Unprinted Texts Preceeded by a General Survey of the Traits of the Negro Song," M.A. thesis 1923, University of California.

254. McCall, Maurice. "Afro-American Music: Let Americans be Proud of Their Musical Heritage," Freeing the Spirit 5 (1977) 6-9.

255. McClendon, William H. "Black Music: Sound and Feeling for Black Liberation," Black Scholar 7 (1976) 20-25.

256. McCue, George, ed. Music in American Society 1776-1976: From Puritan Hymn to Synthesizer. New Brunswick, N.J.: Transaction Books, 1977.

257. McGinty, Doris. "African Tribal Music: A Study of Transition," Journal of Human Relations 8 (1960) 739-748.

258. McNeil, Albert J. "The Social Foundations of the Music of Black Americans," Music Educators Journal 60 (1974) 43-46, 81-82.

259. Mellinger, E. Henry. "Negro Songs from Georgia," Journal of American Folklore 44 (1931) 437.

260. Merriam, Alan P. "The African Idiom in Music," Journal American Folklore 75 (1965) 120-132.

261. _____. "African Music," in Continuity and Change in African Cultures, William Bascom and M. Herskovits, eds. Chicago: University of Chicago Press, 1959, 49-86.

262. Mims, A. Grace. "Soul: The Black Man and His Music," Negro History Bulletin. 33 (1970) 141-146.

263. Moore, Carmen et al. "Black Music: Where It's At and Where It's Going," Africa Report 18 (1973) 12-18, 20-24.

264. Montague, J. Harold."A Historical Survey of Negro Music and Musicians and Their Influence on 20th Century Music," M.A. thesis, 1929, Syracuse University.

265. Moton, Robert. "Negro Folk Music," Southern Workman 44 (1915) 329-350.

266. Murphy, Jeanette Robinson. Southern Thoughts for Northern Thinkers and African Music in America. New York: Bandanna Publishing Company, 1904.

267. _____. "Survival of African Music in America," Appleton's Popular Science Monthly LV (Sept. 1899), n.p.

268. "Negro Folk Songs," Southern Workman 54 (1925) 533.

269. "Negro Music: A Definitive American Expression," Negro History Bulletin 27 (1964) 120-121.

270. Nettl, Bruno. Folk Music in the United States: An Introduction. Detroit: Wayne State University Press, 1976.

271. _____. Folk and Traditional Music of the Western Continents. 2nd ed. Englewood Cliffs, New Jersey: Prentice Hall, Inc., 1973.

272. Niles, John J. "Shout Coon Shout!" Musical Quarterly 16 (1930) 516-530.

273. Nketia, J.H. African Gods and Music. Legon: Institute of African Studies, University of Ghana, 1970.

274. _____. African Music in Ghana. Evanston: Northwestern University Press, 1963.

275. _____. Drumming in Akan Communities of Ghana. London: Thomas Nelson and Sons, Ltd., 1963.

276. _____. "Musicology and African Music: A Review of Problems and Areas of Research," Africa in the Wider World. D. Brokensha, Michael Crowder, eds. New York: Pergamon Press, 1967.

277. _____. "The Problem of Meaning in African Music," Ethnomusicology 6 (1962) 1-7.

278. _____. The Music of Africa. London: Gollancz Publishing Co., 1975.

279. "A Notable Negro Concert," Southern Workman 43 (1914) 381-383.

280. Obatala, J.K. "Soul Music in Africa, Has Charlie Got a Brand New Bag," Black Scholar 2 (1971) 8-12.

281. Odum, Howard. The Negro and His Songs. New York: Negro Universities Press, 1968.

282. The Official Theatrical World of Colored Artists,
National Directory and Guide to Authentic Information of
Musicians, Concert-Artists, Actors, Actresses, Performer and
all Others - Allied with the Profession. New York: The
Theatrical World Publishing Co., 1958.

283. Oliver, Paul. The Blues Tradition. New York: Oak
Publications, 1970.

284. _____. The Meaning of the Blues. New York:
Collier Books, 1965.

285. _____. Savannah Syncopators. New York: Stein
and Day, 1970.

286. Otto, J.S. and A.M. Burns. "Use of Race/Hillbilly
Recordings as Sources for Historical Research; the Problem
of Color Hierarchy among Afro-Americans in the Early 20th
Century," Journal American Folklore 85 (1972) 344-355.

287. Parker, W. J. "Famous Melodies, Own Negro Authorship,
Rare Manuscripts Collected by Maud Cuney Have Reveal Musical
Inheritance of Races from Sixth Century, when Mabel was
Favorite Singer," Musical America (August 9, 1924) n.p.

288. Parrish, Lydia. "Plantation Songs of our Old Negro
Slaves," Country Life (1935) 68-70.

289. Patterson, C.L. "A Different Drum: The Image of The
Negro in the Nineteenth-Century Songster," College Language
Association Journal 8 (1964) 44-50.

290 . Patterson, Lindsay. The Negro in Music and Art. 2nd ed.
New York: Publishers Co., 1969.

291 . Peabody, Charles. "Notes on Negro Music," Southern
Workman 33 (1904) 305-309.

292 . Petrie, Gavin. Black Music. London and New York: Hamlyn,
1974.

293. Phillips, Romeo E. "Black Folk Music: Setting the Record
Straight," Music Educators Journal. Washington, D.C.: 60 (4)
41-45.

294. Pleasants, Henry. "Afro-American Epoch-Emergence of a
New Idiom," Music Educator's Journal 57 (1970) 33-37.

295. Porter, Thomas J. "The Social Roots of Afro-American
Music," Freedomways 2 (1971) 264-271.

296. Ramsey, Frederic J. Been Here and Gone. New Brunswick,
N.J.: Rutgers University Press, 1960.

297. _____. Where the Music Started: A Photographic
Essay. New Brunswick, N.J.: Institute of Jazz Studies, Rutgers
University, 1970.

298. Reagon, Bernice. "Songs of the Civil Rights Movement,
1955 to 1965: A Case Study in Culture History," Ph.D. dissertation, 1975, Howard University.

299. Reyes-Schramm, Adelaida. "The Role of Music in the Black
American-Puerto-Rican Interaction in East Harlem," Ph.D. dissertation, 1975, Columbia University.

300. Rhinehart, Charles. "The Black Impact Upon American
Music," South-Western Musician 42 (1973) 12-13.

301. Roach, Hildred. Black American Music Past and Present.
Boston: Crescendo Publishing Co., 1973.

302. Roberts, John Storm. Black Music of Two Worlds. New York:
Praeger Publishers, 1972.

303. Roberts, John Willie. "The Uses and Function of Afro-
American Folk and Popular Music in the Literature of James
Baldwin," Ph.D. dissertation, 1976, Ohio State University.

304. Rosenwald, P.J. "Voices of City Blacks, Set to Music,"
Wall Street Journal 179 (Oct. 22, 1971) 83-90.

305. Roth, Russell. "Escapism Theory of Negro Music Wrong -
It's Stout Poetry," Minneapolis Star (Feb. 11, 1970) n.p.

306. Rublowsky, John. Black Music in America. New York: Basic
Books, 1971.

307. Scarborough, Dorothy. On the Trail of Negro Folksongs.
Boston: Harvard University Press, 1925.

308. Sidran, Ben. Black Talk. New York: Holt, Rinehart and
Winston, 1971.

309. Slotkin, J.S. "Jazz and Its Forerunners as an Example of
Acculturation," American Sociological Review 8 (1943) 570-576.

310. Southern, Eileen. The Music of Black Americans. New York:
W.W. Norton, 1971.

311. _____. "Needs for Research in Black-American
Music," College Music Symposium 13 (1973) 43-52.

312. _____. "An Origin for the Negro Spiritual,"
Black Scholar 3 (1972) 8-13.

313. _____. "Some Guidelines: Music Research and
the Black Aesthetic," Black World 23 (1973) 4-13.

314. _____. Source Readings in Black American Music.
New York: W.W. Norton, 1971.

315. Spearman, Rawn. "Music and Black Culture," Musart 22
(1969) 30-31, 61-63.

316. Starks, George L. "Black Music in the Sea Islands of
South Carolina: Its Cultural Context-Continuity and Change,"
Ph.D. dissertation, 1973, Wesleyan University.

317. Stevenson, Gordon. "Race Records. Victims of Benign
Neglect in Libraries," Wilson Library Bulletin (Bronx) 50
(1975) 224-232.

318. Still, William Grant. "The Negro Musician in America,"
M.E.N.C. Journal 56 (1970) 100-101, 157, 161.

319. Summers, Lynn S. "African Influence and the Blues: An
Interview with Richard A. Waterman," Living Blues 2 (1971)
30-36.

320. Szwed, John F. "Musical Style and Racial Conflict,"
Phylon 27 (1966) 358-366.

321. _____. "Musical Adaptation Among Afro-Americans," Journal of American Folklore 82 (1969) 112-121.

322. _____. "Negro Music: Urban Renewal" in Our
Living Traditions: An Introduction to American Folklore.
Tristam P. Coffin, ed. New York: Basic Books, 1969.

323. Talley, Thomas Washington. Negro Folk Rhymes, Wise and
Otherwise. Port Washington, New York: Kennikat Press, 1968.

324. Tallmadge, William H. Afro-American Music. Buffalo: New
York State University, 1969.

325. Taubman, Howard. "Negro Music Given at Carnegie Hall,"
The Black Perspective in Music 2 (1974) 207-208.

326. Thieme Darius L. "Negro Folksong Scholarship in the
United States," African Music Journal of African Music
Society 2 (1960) 67-72.

327. Trotter, James M. Music and Some Highly Musical People.
Boston: Lee and Shepard Publishers, 1881; Reprinted New York:
Johnson Reprint Corporation, 1968.

328. Tyler, Robert. "The Musical Culture of Afro-America,"
The Black Scholar 3 (1972) 22-27.

329. Uya, Okon Edet. "The Mind of Slaves as Revealed in Their
Songs: An Interpretative Essay," Current Bibliography on
African Affairs 5 (1972) 3-11.

330. Van Dam, Theodore."The Influence of the West African Songs of Derision in the New World," African Music 1 (1954) 53-56.

331. Wachsman, Klaus. Essays on Music and History in Africa. Evanston: Northwestern University Press, 1971.

332. _____. "Negritude in Music," Composer 19 (1966) 12-16.

333. Warren, Fred. The Music of Africa. Englewood Cliffs, N.J.: Prentice-Hall, 1970.

334. Walden, Jean Elizabeth. "The History, Development and Contributions of the Negro Folk Song," M.M. thesis, 1945, Northwestern University.

335. Walton, Ortiz N. Music, Black, White and Blue; A Sociological Survey of the Use and Misuse of Afro-American Music. New York: William Morrow, 1972.

336. _____. "Some Implications for Afro-American Culture: Rationalism and Western Music," Black World 23 (1973) 54-56.

337. Waterman, Richard A. "African Influence on the Music of the Americas," Acculturation in the Americas Proceedings of the 29th International Congress of Americanists, Sol Tax, ed., Chicago: University of Chicago Press, 1952.

338. _____. "On Flogging a Dead Horse: Lessons Learned From the Africanisms Controversy," Ethnomusicology 7 (1963) 83-97.

339. Weman, Henry. African Music and the Church in Africa. Upssola: Studio Missionalia Upsaliensia, 1960.

340. Whalum, Wendell Phillips. "James Weldon Johnson's Theories and Performance Practices of Afro-American Folksong," Phylon 32 (1971) 383-395.

341. White, Clarence C. "The Musical Genius of the American Negro," Southern Workman 62 (1933) 108-117.

342. White, Lillian A. "The Folksongs of the American Negro and Their Value Today," M.A. thesis, 1925, Columbia University.

343. White, Lorenzo. "The Negro and His Songs," Southern Workman 54 (1925) 527-528.

344. Whiting, Helen. Negro Art, Music and Rhyme. Washington, D.C.: Associated Publishers, Inc., 1938.

345. Wilgus, D.K. "The Future of American Folksong Scholarship," Southern Folklore Quarterly 37 (1973) 315-329.

346. Williams, Thelma A. "Origin and Analysis of Negro Folk-Song," M.S. thesis, 1938, Wayne State University.

347. Wollaschek, Richard. Primitive Music. London: Longmeans Green, 1893.

348. Wood, Mabel Travis. "Community Preservation of Negro Music," Southern Workman 53 (1924) 60-63.

349. Work, John W. "Changing Patterns in Negro Folk Songs," Journal American Folklore Society 62 (1949) 136-143.

350. Work, Monroe N. "Musical Parallelisms," Southern Workman 36 (1907) 106-111.

351. Yellin, Victor. "Music in America, An Anthology from the Landing of the Pilgrims to Close of Civil War 1620-1865," Journal of the American Musicological Society 18 (Summer 1965), n.p.

4

Religious Folksongs: Spirituals, Hymns, Blues, and Gospels

352. Adams, Charles G. "Some Aspects of Black Worship," Journal Church Music 15 (1973) 2-9.

353. African Methodist Episcopal Zion Hymnal. Charlotte, N.C.: A.M.E.Z. Publishing House, 1957.

354. "African Methodist Episcopal Zion Hymnal," The Hymn 10 (1959) 99-100.

355. Alford, Delton L. Music in the Pentecostal Church. Cleveland, Tenn.: Pathway Press, 1977.

356. Allen, Richard. A Collection of Spiritual Songs and Hymns Selected from Various Authors. Philadelphia: John Ormrod, 1801.

357. "Aretha Package a Triumph," Billboard (June 10, 1972) 4-10.

358. Arrowwood, M.D. and T.F. Hamilton. "New Negro Spirituals from Lower South Carolina," Journal of American Folklore 41 (1928) 579-582.

359. Backus, Emma M. "Negro Hymns from Georgia," Journal of American Folklore 10 (1879) 202, 264; 11 (1880) 22.

360. Bailey, Harold. "Behind the Gospel Scene Chicago," Gospel News Journal 2 (1966) 6.

361. Barrett, W.A. "Negro Hymnology," Musical Times 15 (1872) 559-562.

362. Banks, Lacy J. "Gospel Music: A Shout of Black Joy," Ebony (May 1972) 161-168.

363. Barton, William E. "Hymns of the Negro," New England Magazine 19 (1899) 609-624.

364. _____. Old Plantation Hymns; A Collection of
Hitherto Unpublished Melodies of The Slave and Freedman,
With Historical and Descriptive Notes. Boston, N.Y.: Lamson,
Wolfee and Co., 1899.

365. Beckham, Albert Sidney. "The Psychology of Negro
Spirituals," Southern Workman 60 (1931) 391-394.

366. Benson, Louis F. The English Hymn Its Development, and
Use. New York: George H. Doran Co., 1915.

367. Black, Doris. "How Black Churches Became a School for
Singing Stars, Sepia 22 (1973) 70-80.

368. Bontemps, Arna. "Rock Church Rock," Book of Negro Folklore. Langston Hughes, ed. New York: Dodd, Meade and Co. 1944,
313-319.

369. Boyer, Clarence H. "The Gospel Song: A Historical and
Analytical Study," M.A. thesis, 1964, Eastman School of Music.

370. Boyer, Horace C. "An Analysis of Black Church Music
with Examples Drawn from Services in Rochester, New York,"
Ph.D. dissertation 1973, Eastman School of Music, University
of Rochester.

371. _____. "An Analysis of His Contributions:
Thomas A. Dorsey, Father of Gospel Music," Black World 23
(1974) 20-28.

372. Brawley, Benjamin. "The Singing of Spirituals,"
Southern Workman 63 (1934) 209-213.

373. Bronner, Simon. "The Legacy of Rev. Gary Davis," Folk-
scene 2 (1975) 14-16.

374. Brooks, June Delores. "Music in Culture: Black Sacred
Song Style, Slidell, Louisiana, Chicago, Illinois," Ph.D.
dissertation, 1973, Northwestern University.

375. Brown, Marian Tally. "A Resource Manual on the Music of
the Southern Fundamentalist Black Church," Ed. d. dissertation,
1974, Indiana University.

376. Brown, Sterling A. "The Spirituals," Book of Negro
Folklore. Langston Hughes, ed. New York: Dodd, Meade and Co.,
1944, 279-288.

377. Bruce, Dickson D., Jr. And They All Sang Halleluja:
Plain-Folk Camp-Meeting Religion 1800-1845. Knoxville:
University of Texas Press, 1974.

378. Bryant, Melville C. Jr. "Derivation and Development of
American Negro Gospel Songs," Ph.D. dissertation 1963,
University of Indiana.

379. Burt, Jesse C. and Duane Allen. The History of Gospel Music. Nashville, Tenn.: Silverline Music, 1971.

380. Carawan, Guy and Candie. Ain't You Got a Right to the Tree of Life New York: Simon and Schuster, 1966.

381. Christensen, Abigail M. Holmes. "Spirituals and Shouts of Southern Negroes," Journal American Folklore 7 (1894) 183-194.

382. Clar, Mimi. "The Negro Church: Its Influence on Modern Jazz," New York Jazz Review (April 1959) n.p.

383. "Clara Ward - at the Village Vanguard," Jet (December 14, 1961) 60-61.

384. Clark, F.A. The Black Music Maker. Philadelphia: A.M.E. Book Concern, Printers, 1923.

385. Cogdall, Jacqueline D. "An Analytical Study of the Similarities and Differences in American Black Spirituals and Gospel Songs from the Southeast Region of Georgia," M.A. thesis, 1972, U.C.L.A.

386. Cohen, Lily Young. Lost Spirituals. N.Y.: W. Neale, 1928.

387. Cone, James H. The Spirituals and the Blues. New York: Seabury Press, 1972.

388. Cooper, Thomas. The African Pilgrim Hymns. London: Bertrand, 1820.

389. Cornell, Jean Guy. Mahalia Jackson, Queen of Gospel Song. Champaign, Ill.: Garrard Publishing Co., 1974.

390. Crane, Harnette Louise. "A Study of African Negro Music and Its Use in the Christ Church in Africa," S.M.M. thesis, 1947, Union Theological Seminary.

391. Dawson, William L. "Interpretation of the Religious Folk-Songs of the American Negro," Etude 73 (1955) n.p.

392. "Desecration of Spirituals," Southern Workman 51 (1922) 501.

393. Dett, R. Nathaniel. "Book of American Negro Spirituals," Southern Workman 54 (1925) 563-565.

394. _____. "St. Helena Island Spiritual," Southern Workman 54 (1925) 527.

395. Dickinson, Eleanor and Barbara Benziger. Revival! New York: Harper and Row, 1974.

396. Dillard, James A. " Developing Music Activities with
Emphasis Especially at the Concord Baptist Church of Christ,
Brooklyn, New York," Ed.d. dissertation, 1951, Teacher's
College, Columbia University.

397. Dixon, Christa R. Negro Spirituals from Bible to Folksongs. Philadelphia: Fortress Press, 1976.

398. Dixon, Robert M.S. and John Godrich. Blues and Gospel
Records: 1902-1942. London: Storyville Publications, 1969.

399. Dorsey, Thomas A. "Dorsey's Songs With A Message,"
Schomburg Collection, New York City Public Library. n.d.

400. Downes, Olin. "Estimates of Dett's 'THE ORDERING OF
MOSES'", Southern Workman 66 (1937) 304-310.

401. Downey, James. "Dr. Watts and Mahalia Jackson (the
Development, Decline and Survival of a Folk Style in America),"
Ethnomusicology 5 (1961) 95-99.

402. _____. "The Gospel Hymn (1875-1930)," M.A.
thesis, 1963, University of Southern Mississippi.

403. _____. "Frontiers of Baptist Hymnody," Church
Musician 15 (1964) n.p.

404. _____. "Rivalism, the Gospel Songs and Social
Reform," Ethnomusicology 9 (1965) 115-125.

405. Duckett, Alfred. "An Interview With Thomas A. Dorsey,"
Black World. 23 (1974) 4-18.

406. Dyen, Doris Jane. "The Role of Shape-Note Singing in the
Musical Culture of Black Communities in Southeast Alabama,"
Ph.D. dissertation, 1977, University of Illinois at Urbana-
Champaign.

407. "Edwin Hawkins Singers," Sepia (August 1969) 66-68.

408. Elmer, Richard M. "Modern Evangelism and Church Music,"
The Hymn 7 (1956) 13-17.

409. Ekwueme, Lazarus. "African Music in Christian Liturgy:
the Igbo Experiment," African Music 3 (1974) 12-33.

410. Emerson, William C. Stories and Spirituals of the Negro
Slave. Boston: Gorman, 1930.

411. Epstein, Dena J. Sinful Tunes & Spirituals: Black Folk
Music in The Civil War. Chicago: University of Illinois
Press, 1977.

412. Eskew, Harry. "A Cultural Understanding of Hymnody,"
The Hymn 23 (1972) 70-84

413. Evans, Arthur Lee. "The Development of the Negro
Spiritual as Choral Art Music by Afro-American Composers
with Annotated Guide to the Performance of Selected
Spirituals," Ph.D. dissertation, 1972, University of Miami.

414. Evans, David. "Black Religious Music," Journal of American Folklore 83 (1970) 472-480.

415. Fisher, Miles Mark. Negro Slave Songs in the United
States. Ithaca: Cornell University Press, 1953.

416. "Fisk Singers Abroad," Southern Workman 56 (1927) 196.

417. Friedel, L.M. The Bible and The Negro Spirituals. St.
Louis: St. Augustine Seminary, 1947.

418. "G.D. Pike," The American Missionary 39 (1885) 68.

419. Gaber, Deborah R. "Negro Spirituals and Recent Black
Soul Music: A Comparative Study," M.A. thesis, 1972, Indiana
University.

420. Garon, Paul. "Blues and the Church: Revolt and Resigna-
tion," Living Blues 1 (1970) 18-23.

421. Gentry, Linnell. A History and Encyclopedia of Country
Western and Gospel Music. 2nd ed, Nashville: Claremont Corp.
1969.

422. Gilchrest, Anne G. "The Folk Element in Early Revival
Hymns and Tunes," Journal Folk-Song Society 8 (1928) 61-95.

423. "Gloria Spencer 570 lb. Gospel Queen," Sepia (April 1969)
52-54.

424. Godrich, John and Robert M.W. Dixon. Blues and Gospel
Records 1902-1942. London: Storyville Publications and Co.,
1969.

425. Gold, Charles E. "The Gospel Song: Contemporary Opinion,"
The Hymn 9 (1958) 69-73.

426. _____. "A Study of the Gospel Song," M.M.
thesis, 1953, University of Southern California.

427. Gordon, Robert Winslow. "Negro 'Shouts' from Georgia,"
New York Times Magazine (April 24, 1927) n.p.

428. Gordeau, Laurraine. Just Mahalia, Baby. Waco, Texas:
Ward Books, 1975.

429. "Gospel Music," Downbeat 9th Yearbook (1964) n.p.

430. "Gospel Music Association," Billboard (April 1969) 54-56.

431. "Gospel Music Holds It's Own," Gospel News Journal 5 (1968) 2.

432. "Gospel Music in the United States," in The Negro Almanac. Harry A. Ploski and Warren Marr, II, eds. New York: Bellwether Co., 1976, 977-978.

433. Gospel Pearls. Nashville: Sunday School Publishing Board, 1921.

434. "Gospel to Pop to Gospel," Ebony (July, 1962) 107-108.

435. "Gospel Singers," Ebony (December, 1950) 91-95.

436. "Gospel Singers in Coffee Houses," Sepia (March, 1960) 60-64.

437. "Gospel Singers - Pop Up, Sweet Chariot," Time (May 24, 1963) 48.

438. "The Gospelers," Time (June 15, 1962) 64.

439. Grady, Edythe R. "Sacred Music of the Negro in the U.S.A." M.S.M. thesis, 1950, Union Theological Seminary.

440. Greene, Barbara. "African Music Survivals in the Songs of the Negro in Haiti, Jamaica and the U.S.," M.A. thesis, 1956, University of Chicago.

441. Griffin, George H. "The Slave Music of the South," American Missionary Magazine 36 (1882) 70-72.

442. Grissom, Mary Allen. The Negro Sings a New Heaven. New York: Dover Publications, 1969.

443. Grossman, Stefan, ed. Rev. Gary Davis/Holy Blues. New York: Robbins Music Corp., 1970.

444. _____. "A Rare Interview with Rev. Gary Davis," Sing-Out! 23 (1974) 2-5, 36, 46.

445. "Fisk Jubilee Singers," Sepia (July 1964) 24-27.

446. Hall, Claude. "Negro Gospel," Billboard (October 23, 1965) 44-53.

447. Hammond, Paul Garnett. "Music in Urban Revivalism in the Northern United States, 1800-1835," D.M.A. dissertation, 1974, Southern Baptist Theological Seminary.

448. "Hampton Institute Choir," Southern Workman 56 (1927) 53-54.

449. "Hampton Institute Choir," Southern Workman 58 (1929) 158-160.

450. Hartley, Kenneth. Bibliography of Thesis and Dissertations in Sacred Music. Detroit: Information Coordinators, 1966.

451. Haslam, Gerald W. "Two Traditions in Afro-American Literature," Research Studies 37 (1969) 31-36.

452. Hatfield, Edwin F. Freedom's Lyre: Or, Psalms, Hymns, and Sacred Songs for the Slave and His Friends. New York: S.W. Benedict, 1840.

453. Hawkins, Floyd W. Hallelujah, Unique Gospel Songs and Spirituals. Kansas City, Mo.: Lillenas Publishing Co., 1958.

454. Hayes, Cedric. J. A Discography of Gospel Records 1937-1971. Copenhagen: Karl Emil Knudsen, 1973.

455. Hayes, Roland. My Songs; Afroamerican Religious Folk Song. Boston: Little: Brown, 1948.

456. Hirlbit, Tony. The Gospel Sound: Good News and Bad Times. New York: Simon and Schuster, 1971.

457. Hepburn, D. "Big Bonanza in Gospel Music," Sepia (March, 1963) 13-18.

458. Hiemm, M. "An Introduction to Gospel Music," Blues (November, 1968) 18-25.

459. Hill, Edwin. A Brief Sketch of the Career of Edwin Hill, Composer and Publisher of Music with Catalogue. Philadelphia: A.M.E. Book Concern, n.d.

460. Hobson, Charles. "The Gospel Truth," Down Beat. (May, 1968) 17-20.

461. Hollingworth, R. "God Rock," Melody Maker (February, 1971) 9.

462. Hughes, Langston. "Gospel Singing: When The Spirit Really Moves," The Sunday Herald Tribune Magazine (October, 1963) n.p.

463. Hulan, Richard. "Folk Hymns: The Cane Ridge Legacy," Festival of American Folklife. Washington, D.C.: Smithsonian Institution, 1973, 18-20.

464. The Hymnbook of the A.M.E. Church. Philadelphia: Publishing Dept. of A.M.E. Church, 1873.

465. Jackson, George Pullen. "The Genesis of the Negro Spiritual," American Mercury 26 (1932) 243-248.

466. Jackson, George Pullen. "Buckwheat Notes," Musical Quarterly 19 (1933) 393-401.

467. Jackson, Irene V. "Afro-American Gospel Music and Its
Social Setting with Special Attention to Roberta Martin,"
Ph.D. dissertation, 1974, Wesleyan University.

468. Jackson, Jesse. Make a Joyful Noise Unto the Lord. The
Life of Mahalia Jackson. New York: Thomas Y. Crowell, 1974.

469. Jackson-Brown, Irene V. "Afro-American Sacred Song in
the Nineteenth Century: A Survey of a Neglected Source," The
Black Perspective in Music 4 (1976) 22-38.

470. John, Janheinz. "The Negro Spiritual," Neo-African
Literature: A History of Black Writing, translated by Oliver
Coburn and Ursula Lehrburger. New York: Grove, 1969, 155-165.

471. "James Cleveland, Top U.S. Gospel Artist," Sepia (May,
1965) 54-59.

472. James, Willis L. "The Romance of the Negro Folk Cry in
America," Phylon 16 (1955) 15-30.

473. Johnson, Guy B. Folk. "The Negro Spiritual, a Problem
in Anthropology," American Anthropologist 33 (1931) 157-171.

474. Johnson, James. "The Negro Spiritual: Its Form - and Its
Uses in Worship," M.S.M. thesis, 1968 Union Theological
Seminary.

475. Jones, Solomon and Paul Tanner. "Afro-American Music:
Black Moans," Music Journal 28 (1970) 36-37.

476. "Jubilee Singers," American Missionary 34 (1880) 291.

477. "The Jubilee Singers - A Good Use of Negro Suffrage,"
American Missionary 32 (1878) 5.

478. "Jubliee Singers: Success in Great Britain," American
Missionary 20 (1876) 37.

479. Keith, Gwendolyn Edwards. "The Status of Negro Church
Youth Choirs in the State of Ohio," M.A. thesis 1950, Ohio
State University.

480. Kelly, Raymond. "Gospel Music and Its Use in Three
Urban Churches," B.D. thesis, 1968, School of Religion,
Howard University.

481. Kennedy, Walter E., III. "Gospel: A Living Musical
Tradition," 1973 Festival of American Folklife. Washington,
D.C.: Smithsonian Institution, 1973, 46-47.

482. Kerr, Thomas Henderson. "A Critical Survey of Printed
Vocal Arrangements of Afro-American Religious Folk Songs,"
M.M. thesis, 1939, Eastman School of Music, University of
Rochester.

483. Ketcham, George F. "Hampton Choir and Quartette,"
Southern Workman 60 (1931) 51-59.

484. King, Dearence E. "A Comparative Study of a Group of
Standard Hymns and Gospel Songs," M.A. thesis, 1940, Howard
University.

485. "King of the Gospel Song Writers (Thomas A. Dorsey),"
Ebony (November, 1962) 122-127.

486. Kirby, Percival. "A Study of Negro Harmony," Musical
Quarterly 16 (July, 1930) 404-414.

487. Kurath, Gertrude. "Rhapsodies of Salvation: Negro
Responsory Hymns," Southern Folklore Quarterly 23 (1956)
178-182.

488. Lawrence, Arthur K. Jr. "The Problem of Music in the
Negro Church," M.A. thesis, 1947, Ohio State University.

489. Leiser, Willie. "The Negro Spiritual and Gospel Festival
of 1966," Gospel News Journal 2 (March 1966) 1-5.

490. Lewis, Thelma Marguerite. "Twenty-Five Negro Spirituals
Arranged for Use in Schools with Explanatory Notes and
Illustrations," M.M.E. thesis, 1950, Boston University.

491. Lindermann, Bill. "An Introduction to Black Gospel
Music," Living Blues 2 (1971) 21-22.

492. Logan, Robert Barr. "The Negro Spiritual: A Study of
the Spiritual and an Evaluation of the Place in the Music of
the Lutheran Church," B.D. thesis, 1950, Lutheran Theological
Seminary.

493. Long, Norman G. "The Theology and Psychology of the
Negro's Religion Prior to 1860 as Shown Particularly in the
Spiritual," M.A. thesis, 1956, Oberlin.

494. Louw, Johan K. "African Music in Christian Worship,"
African Music: Journal African Music Society 2 (1958) 51-53.

495. Lovell, John Jr. Black Song: The Forge and The Flame:
The Story of How the Afro-American Spiritual was Hammered
Out. New York: Macmillan, 1972.

496. McCarroll, Jessee C. "Black Influence on Southern White
Protestant Church Music During Slavery," Ed. dissertation,
1972, Columbia University.

497. McKinley, Frank Arnold. "The American Gospel Song,"
M.A. thesis, 1946, Westminster Choir College.

498. McKissick, Marvin. "The Function of Music in American
Revivals Since 1875," The Hymn 9 (1958) 107-117.

499. McLaughlin, Wayman B. "Symbolism and Mysticism in the
Spirituals," Phylon 24 (1963) 69-77.

500. Margaret Aikins. "God Talks to My Heart Through Songs,"
Sepia 13 (1964) 53-57.

501. Marshall, Howard Wright."'Open Up Them Pearly Gates'
Pattern and Religious Expression in Bluegrass Gospel Music,"
Folklore Forum 4 (1971) 92-112.

502. Mary, Sister Esther. "Spirituals in the Church,"
Southern Workman 63 (1934) 308-314.

503. Maultsby, Portia K. "Afro-American Religious Music 1619-
1861. Part I - Historical Development; Part II - Computer
Analysis of One Hundred Spirituals," Ph.D. dissertation, 1974,
University of Wisconsin.

504. _____. "Music of Northern Independent Black
Churches During the Ante-Bellum Period," Ethnomusicology
19 (1975) 401-420.

505. _____. "Black Spirituals: An Analysis of
Textual Forms and Structures," The Black Perspective in
Music 4 (1976) 54-69.

506. Merritt, Nancy G. "Negro Spirituals in American Collections; a Handbook for Students Studying Negro Spirituals,"
M.A. thesis, 1940, Howard University.

507. Michaux, Lightfoot Solomon. Spiritual Happiness Making
Songs, Compiled and Sung and Published by Michaux. Washington,
D.C.: Author, n.d. (Moreland-Springarn Collection, Howard
University).

508. "Misuse of Name of Hampton Singers," American Missionary
20 (1876) 246.

509. Moore, Ella Sheppard. "The Original Jubilee Singers,"
The American Missionary 56 (August 1902).

510. Moore, LeRoy, Jr. "The Spiritual: Soul of Black Religion,"
Church History 40 (1971) 79-81.

511. "National Black Gospel Meet Draws 8,000; D.J.'s Active,
Billboard (September 2, 1972) 1.

512. Neil, Bobby Joe. "Philip B.P. Bliss (1838-1876): Gospel
Hymn Composer and Compiler," Ed.D. dissertation, 1977,
Baptist Theological Seminary.

513. "Negro Spiritual Contest in Columbia," Southern Workman
55 (1926) 372-373.

514. Newton, Francis. "Gospel Song," New Statesman (April 11,
1959) 504-505.

515. Odum, Adrue (Armstrong). The Hall of Fame of Contemporary Contributors to Gospel Music. Washington, D.C.: author, 1947. (Music division, Library of Congress).

516. "Origin of the Negro Spirituals," Negro History Bulletin 25 (1962) 179-180.

517. Owens, Garfield. All God's Children. Nashville, New York: Abingdon Press, 1971.

518. Patterson, Floyd H., Jr. "The Southern Baptist Sunday School Board's Program of Church Music," Ph.D. dissertation, 1957, George Peabody College for Teachers.

519. Paul, June Delores Brooks. "Music in Culture: Black Sacred Song Style, Slidell, Louisiana," Ph.D. dissertation, 1973, Northwestern University.

520. Peach, Everett. "The Gospel Songs: Its Influence on Christian Hymnody," M.A. thesis, 1960, Wayne State.

521. Pearson, Bill. "God Don't Never Change: A View of Pre-War Gospel Music," Blues World 45 (1973) 3-6.

522. Phenix, George P. "Religious Folksongs of the Negro," Southern Workman 56 (1927) 151-152.

523. Phillips, Romeo E. "White Racism in Black Church Music," Negro History Bulletin 36 (1973) 17-20.

524. _____. "A Selected, Annotated Discography: Dorsey Songs on Record," Black World 23 (1974) 29-32.

525. Pinkston, Alfred Adolphus. "Lined Hymns, Spirituals, and the Associated Lifestyle of Rural Black People in the United States," Ph.D. dissertation, 1975, University of Miami.

526. "Popularity of the Spirituals," Southern Workman 55 (1926) 149-150.

527. Powell, A.C. "Rocking the Gospel Train," Negro Digest 9 (1951) 10-13.

528. "The Power of Gospel Music," Gospel News Journal 5 (1968) 4, 6, 10, 14.

529. "Putting a Ban on Spirituals (Protest Against Singing Spirituals in Amusement Halls and Theaters)," Southern Workman 52 (1928) 384.

530. Raichelson, Richard M. "Black Religious Folksong: A Study in Generic and Social Change," Ph.D. dissertation, 1975, University of Pennsylvania.

531. "Revival at the Bars," Newsweek (Sept. 7, 1970) 53.

532. Ricks, George Robinson. Some Aspects of the Religious
Music of the U.S. Negro: An Ethnomusicological Study with
Special Emphasis on the Gospel Tradition. Ph.D. dissertation,
1960, Northwestern University.

533. _____. Some Aspects of the Religious Music of
the United States Negro. Richard Dorson, ed. New York: Arno
Press, 1977.

534. Riedel, Johannes. Soul Music Black and White. The Influence of Black Music on the Churches. Minneapolis: Augsburg
Publishing House, 1975.

535. "Roberta Martin Singers," Gospel News Journal 3 (1966) 5.

536. Robinson, John W. "A Song, A Shout, and a Prayer," in
The Black Experience in Religion. C. Eric Lincoln, ed. New
York: Anchor Books, 1974, 212-235.

537. Rodeheaver, Homer. Singing Black (Twenty Thousand Miles
with a Music Missionary). Chicago: Rodeheaver Company, 1936.

538. Rookmaaker, H.R. "Let's Sing the Old Dr. Watts: A
Chapter in the History of Negro Spirituals," The Gordon
Review 9 (1966) n.p.

539. Sallee, James. A History of Evangelistic Hymnody. Grand
Rapids, Michigan: Baker Book House, 1977.

540. Saminsky, Lazare. Music of the Ghetto and the Bible.
New York: A.M.S. Press, 1977.

541. Sankey, Ira D. Sankey's Story of the Gospel Hymns and
of Sacred Songs and Solos. Philadelphia: Sunday School Times
Co., 1906.

542. Sankey, Ira D., et. al. Gospel Hymns. 6 vols. New York:
Da Capa, 1977.

543. Schimmel, Johannes C. Spirituals and Gospelsongs.
Gelnhausen: Burckhardthaus-Verlag, 1963.

544. Simoneaux, M.S. "An Evaluation of the Baptist Hymnal
(1956) in Comparison with Five Hymnals Previously Popular
Among Southern Baptists from 1904 until 1956," Ed.d. dissertation, 1970, New Orleans Baptist Theological Seminary.

545. Sims, John Norman. "The Hymnody of the Camp Meeting
Tradition," S.M.D. dissertation, 1960, Union Theological
Seminary.

546. "The Singers to the Missionaries, Meeting," American
Missionary 1 (1878) 180.

547. "Singing for Sinners," Newsweek (September 2, 1957) 86.

548. Small, Katherine Lucille. "The Influence of the Gospel Song on the Negro Church," M.A. thesis, 1945, Ohio State University.

549. Smoot, Maggie Wilson. "Logbook of Travels (1882-89) of Fish Jubilee Singers," Moreland-Springarn Collection, Howard University.

550. Southall, Geneva. "Black Composers and Religious Music," Black Perspective in Music 2 (1974) 45-50.

551. Southern, Eileen. "An Origin for the Negro Spiritual?" The Black Scholar 3 (1972) 8-13.

552. _____. "Musical Practices in Black Churches of Philadelphia and New York, ca. 1800-1844," Journal of the American Musicological Society 30 (Summer 1977) 296-312.

553. Spence, M.E. "The Jubilee of Jubilees at Fisk University," Southern Workman 51 (1922) 73-80.

554. "From Spiritual to Vaudeville," Journal of American Folklore 35 (1922) 331.

555. "Spirituals," Nineteenth Century Sheet Music Collection, Southern Baptist Theological Seminary.

556. "Staple Singers Sell Soul With a Gospel Beat," Jet (December, 1971) 51-59.

557. "Staple Singers; Soul Family," Sepia (December, 1968) 54-58.

558. Stearns, Marshall. "If You Want to Go to Heaven, Shout," High Fidelity (August 1959) 36-38.

559. Stone, Michael K. "Heav'n Rescued Land: American Hymns and American Destiny," Journal of Popular Culture 10 (1976) 133-141.

560. Sutherland, S. "Dionne's Father Espouses Black Gospel's Influence," Billboard (January 3, 1972) 44.

561. "The Sunday-School Concert," American Missionary 33 (1879) 70.

562. Swetnam, G. "The Church Hymn as a Folklore Form," Keystone Folklore Quarterly 9 (1964) 144-153.

563. Talbot, Edith. "True Religion in Negro Hymns," The Southern Workman 51 (1922) 63-86.

564. Tallmadge, William H. "Dr. Watts and Mahalia Jackson - The Development, Decline, and Survival of a Folk Style in America," Ethnomusicology 5 (1961) 95-99.

565. _____ ."The Responsorial and Antiphonal Practice in Gospel Song," Ethnomusicology 12 (1958) 219-238.

566. Taylor, J.E. "The Sociological, and Psychological Implications of the Texts of the Antebellum Negro Spirituals," Ed.d. dissertation, 1971, University of Northern Colorado.

567. _____ . "Somethin' On My Mind: A Cultural and Historical Interpretation of Spiritual Texts," Ethnomusicology 19 (1975) 387-400.

568. Taylor, Marshall W. A Collection of Revival Hymns and Plantation Melodies. Cincinnati: Marshall Taylor and W.C. Echols, 1882.

569. Terrell, C.S. "Spirituals from Alabama," Journal American Folklore 43 (1930) 322-324.

570. "Thomas A. Dorsey," Living Blues 20 (1975) 16-34.

571. Thompson, Era Bell. "Love Comes to Mahalia," Ebony (November, 1969) 50-61.

572. _____ . "When Mahalia Sings, Ebony (January, 1954) 35-58.

573. Thrower, Sarah Selina. "The Spiritual of the Gullah Negro in South Carolina," M.A. thesis, 1954, Cincinnati Conservatory of Music.

574. Tiegel, Eliot. "From Prayer House to Plush Nightclub," Billboard (October 23, 1965) 44.

575. Tindley, Charles Albert. New Songs of Paradise. Philadelphia: Paradise Publishing Co., 1916.

576. "A Tribute to Hampton Choir," Southern Workman 56 (1927) 506.

577. "A Tribute to Negro Spirituals," Southern Workman 55 (1926) 397.

578. Turner, Beatrice Seberia. "The Effectiveness of Arrangements in Negro Spirituals," M.A. thesis, 1947, Ohio State.

579. Turner, Lucille Price. "Negro Spirituals in the Making," Musical Quarterly 17 (1931) 480-485.

580. Vance, Joel. "Gospel Can Set You Free," New York Times (March 12, 1972) 2.

581. "Voices of Hope," Sepia (December, 1961) 76-78.

582. Walker, Wyatt Tee. "The Soulful Journey of the Negro Spiritual," Negro Digest 12 (1963) 84-95.

583. _____. "The Musical Tradition of Afro-Ameri-
cans and Its Relationship to and Influences on Social Change,"
D.Min. dissertation, 1975, Martin Luther King Program,
Colgate-Rochester Divinity School.

584. Whalum, Wendell P. "James Weldon Johnson's Theories and
Performance Practices of Afro-American Folksong," Phylon
32 (1971) 383-395.

585. _____. "The Spiritual as Mature Choral Com-
position," Black World 23 (1974) 34-39.

586. Wardlow, Gayle Dean. "Rev. D.C. Rice-Gospel Singer,"
Storyville 23 (June, July 1969) 164-167, 183.

587. Warrick, Mancal and Joan Hillsman. The Progress of
Gospel Music. New York: Vantage, 1977.

588. Washington, Joseph R. "Negro Spirituals," The Hymn 15
(1964) 101-110.

589. Waterman, Richard A. "Gospel Hymns of a Negro Church in
Chicago," International Folk Music Council 3 (1951) 87-93.

590. Watkins, Patricia D. "Origins of and Influences Upon
Black Slave Spirituals, The Validity of Two Schools of
Thought," Ba Shiru (Fall 1970-Spring 1971) 94-102.

591. Westerman, W. Scott. "The Term 'Gospel Hymn,'" The
Hymn 9 (1958) 61-62.

592. Wilgus, D.K. "Gospel Songs," Journal of American Folklore. 79 (1966) 510-515.

593. Williams, B. "Gospel Pubs in Drive for Rights," Billboard
(October 23, 1971) 2.

594. _____. "Integrated Atlanta Meeting Forming Black
Gospel Association," Billboard (November 13, 1971) 1-3.

595. _____. "First Integrated Gospel Act," Billboard
(February 26, 1972) 3-4

596. Williams-Jones, Pearl. "Afro-American Gospel Music,"
in Development of Materials For a One Year Course in African
Music for the General Undergraduate Student. Vada E. Butcher,
ed. Washington, D.C.: H.E.W., Office of Education, 1970,
199-239.

597. _____. "Afro-American Gospel Music: A Crystalli-
zation of the Black Aesthetic," Ethnomusicology 19 (1975)
373-385.

598. _____. "Performance Style in Black Gospel
Music," in Black People and Their Culture, Linn Shapiro, ed.
Washington: Smithsonian Institution, 1976, 26-41.

599. Williams, Martin. "Gospel at the Box Office," <u>Saturday</u>
<u>Review</u> (August, 1963) 41.

600. Williams, Robert. "Preservation of the Oral Tradition of
Singing Hymns in Negro Religious Music," Ph.D. dissertation,
1973, Florida State University.

601. Williford, Doxie. "A Discography of Mississippi Negro
Vocal Blues, Gospels and Folk Music," M.A. thesis, 1968,
University of Mississippi.

602. Work, John Wesley. "Plantation Meistersinger," <u>Musical</u>
<u>Quarterly</u> 27 (1941) 97-106.

603. _____. "Changing Patterns in Negro Folksongs,"
<u>Journal American Folklore</u> 62 (1949) 136-142.

604. Young, M. "Clara Ward: the Little Giant of Gospel Music,"
<u>Sepia</u> (January, 1960) 46-49.

605. Baker, Barbara Wesley. "Black Gospel Music Styles, 1942-
1975: Analysis and Interpretation for Music Education,"
Ph.D. dissertation, 1978, University of Maryland.

5

Black Church/Black Religion

606. Adams, Samuel C. "The Acculturation of the Delta Negro," in Mother Wit from the Laughing Barrel, Alan Dundes, ed. Englewood Cliffs, N.J.: Prentice-Hall, Inc. 1973, 515-522.

607. Alho, Olli. The Religion of the Slaves: A Study of the Religious Tradition and Behavior of Plantation Slaves in the United States 1830-1865. Helsinki: Suomalainen Tiedeakatemia Academia Scientiarum Fennica, 1976.

608. Battle, Allen O. Status and Personality in a Negro Holiness Sect. Washington, D.C.: Associated Publishers, 1961.

609. "The Black Religious Tradition," in The Negro Almanac, Harry A. Ploski and Warren Marr,   eds. New York: Bell-wether Co., 1976, 945-978.

610. Boaz, R. "My Thirty Years With Father Divine," Ebony 20 (1965) 88-90.

611. Boisen, Anton T. "Economic Distress and Religious Experience: A Study of the Holy Rollers," Psychiatry 2 (1939) 185-194.

612. Bourguignon, Erika, and Louanna Pettray. "Spirit Possession, Trance and Cross Cultural Research," Symposium on New Approaches to the Study of Religion, (Proceedings of the 1964 Annual Spring Meeting of the American Ethnological Society), Seattle: University of Washington Press, 1964.

613. Bourguignon, Erika. "The Self, the Beahavorial Environment, and the Theory of Spirit Possession," Context and Meaning in Cultural Anthropology, Melford E. Spiro, ed. New York: The Free Press, 1965.

614. _____. "Afro-American Religion: Tradition and Transformations," in Black America, John F. Szwed, ed. New York: Basic Books, 1970, 190-204.

615. Bryant, M. Winifred. "Negro Services," American Missionary 46 (1892) 301-302.

616. Burt, W.C. "The Baptist Ox," Journal of American Folklore
34 (1921) 397-398.

617. Carter, Harold A. The Prayer Tradition of Black People.
Valley Forge, Pa.: Judson, 1976.

618. Childs, D.T. "A Foundational Approach to Music in Worship
Based on Rudolf Otto's Das Heilige," Ph.D. dissertation, 1971,
George Peabody College for Teachers.

619. Catton, W.R. "What Kind of People Does a Religious Cult
Attract?" American Sociological Review 22 (1957) 561-566.

620. "Church and the Homosexual," Sepia (June, 1967) 68-69.

621. Clark, E. The Small Sects in America. New York: Abingdon,
1949.

622. Dana, M. "Voodoo, Its Effect on the Negro Race,"
Metropolitan Magazine 27 (1908) 529-538.

623. Daniel, Vattel E. "Ritual in Chicago's South Side
Churches for Negroes," Ph.D. dissertation, 1940, University
of Chicago.

624. _____. "Ritual and Stratification in Chicago
Negro Churches," American Sociological Review 7 (1941) 352-
361.

625. Davenport, Frederick M. Primitive Traits in Religious
Revivals: A Study in Mental and Social Evolution. New York:
McMillan Co., 1906.

626. Davidson, J.R. "A Dictionary of Protestant Church
Music," D.S.M. dissertation, 1971, Southern Baptist Theological Seminary.

627. Davis, Henderson. "The Religious Experience Underlying
the Negro Spiritual," Ph.D. dissertation, 1950, Boston
University.

628. Dillard, J.L. "On the Grammar of Afro-American Naming
Practices," Mother Wit from the Laughing Barrell, Alan Dundes,
ed. Englewood Cliffs: Prentice-Hall, 1973, 175-181.

629. Divers, Jesseyca Pauline. "The African Methodist
Episcopal Church and Its Hymnal," M.M. thesis, 1944, Northwestern University.

630. Duckett, A. "Church of God in Christ: Church that is
Run Like a Theatre," Sepia (February, 1960) 52-56.

631. Ellison, J. Malais. "The Negro Church in Rural Virginia,"
Southern Workman 60 (1931) 67-73; 176-178; 201-210.

632. "Exhortation (A Negro Sermon)," Century 1 (1912) 58-59.

633. Faulkner, William J. "Influence of Folklore Upon Religious Experience of Ante-Bellum Negro," Journal Religious
Thought 24 (1968) 26-28.

634. Fauset, Arthur H. Black Gods of the Metropolis. Philadelphia: University of Pennsylvania Press, 1944.

635. Ferris, William R. "The Rose Hill Service," Mississippi
Folklore Register 6 (1972) 37-56.

636. Fickler, Joseph H. "American Religion and the Negro,"
The Negro American. Boston: Talcott Parsons, Houghton Mifflin
Co., 1966, 401-417.

637. Fisher, Miles Mark. "History of Olivet Baptist Church
of Chicago," M.A. thesis, 1922, University of Chicago.

638. _____. "Organized Religion and the Cults,"
Crisis 44 (1937) 8-10, 29.

639. Forbes, James A. "Pentecostal Insights for Black Church
Empowerment," D.Min., 1975, Martin Luther King Program,
Colgate-Rochester Divinity School.

640. Frazier, E. Franklin. "A Folk Culture in the Making,"
Southern Workman 57 (1928) 197-199.

641. _____. The Negro Church in America. New York:
Schocken Books, 1963.

642. George, Carol. Segregated Sabbaths. New York: Oxford
University Press, 1973.

643. Glenn, Norval D. "Negro Religion and Negro Status in
the United States," in Religion, Culture, and Society, Louis
Schieder, ed. New York: Wiley, 1964, 156-173.

644. Goodwin, Reverend W.T. "From Easter Sunrise Sermon,"
Alcheringa 4 (1975) 1-14.

645. Hall, Ernest. "A Negro Institutional Church," Southern
Workman 50 (1921) 113-118.

646. Hollenwager, Walter. Pentecostals: The Charismatic
Movement in the Churches. New York: Augsburg, 1972.

647. Holt, Arthur. "Case Records as Data for Studying the
Conditioning of Religious Experience by Social Factors,"
American Journal Sociology (1926) 227-236.

648. Holt, Grace Sims. "Stylin' Outta the Black Pulpit,"
Rappin' and Stylin' Out. Thomas Kockman, ed. Urbana: University
of Illinois Press, 1972, 189-204.

649. Holt, John B. "Holiness Religion: Cultural Shock and
Social Reorganization," American Sociological Review 5 (1940)
211-236.

650. Houser, Susie A. "A Community-Serving Church," (Olivet
Baptist) Chicago," Southern Workman 54 (1923) 58-64.

651. Hudson, Winthrop S. "Shouting Methodists," Encounter
29 (1968) 33-45.

652. Hurston, Zora Neal. "Shouting," in Negro Anthology,
Nancy Cunard, ed. London: Cunard at Wishart and Co., 1934,
44-50.

653. James, William. The Varieties of the Religious Experience
New York: The Modern Library, 1902.

654. Johnson, Charles A. "The Frontier Camp-Meeting: Contemporary and Historical Appraisals, 1805-1840," Mississippi
Valley Historical Review 37 (1950) n.p.

655. Johnson, Joseph A. The Soul of a Black Preacher. Philadelphia: Pilgrim Press, 1971.

656. Jones, Raymond. "A Comparative Study of Religious Cult
Behavior Among Negroes with Special Reference to Emotional
Conditioning Factors," B.D. thesis, 1939, Howard University.

657. Kaufman, Helen L. From Jehovah to Jazz. New York: Dodd,
1937.

658. Kavolis, V. "Church Involvement and Marital Status as
Restraints on Nonconforming Sexual Behavior," American
Sociological Review 11 (1962) 132-139.

659. King, C.H. "The Dying Art of Shouting," Negro Digest
12 (1962) 21-26.

660. King, W.H. "Apostolic Preaching and Responsibility for
Our Time," Journal of Religious Thought 26 (Summer, 1968)
57-69.

661. Kreugen, E.T. "Negro Religious Expression," American
Journal of Sociology 38 (1932) 22-31.

662. Kyles, Bishop L.W. "The Contributions of the Negro the
Religious Life of America," Journal Negro History 2 (1926)
8-16.

663. Leslie, Charles ed. Anthropology of Folk Religion. New
York: Vintage Books, 1960.

664. Lewis, I.M. Ecstatic Religion: An Anthropological Study of Spirit Possession and Shamanism Middlesex, England: Penguin Books, 1971.

665. Lincoln, C. Eric. "Key Man of the South: The Negro Minister," New York Times Magazine. July 12, 1964, 43-61.

666. _____. ed. The Black Experience in Religion. New York: Anchor Books, 1974.

667. Lockwood, J. Palmer. Darkey Sermons from Charleston County. Columbia, S.C.: The State Co., 1925.

668. Lomax, Ruby Terrill. "Negro Baptizing," Texas Folklore Society Publication 19 (1944) 1-8.

669. Long, Charles H. "Perspectives for a Study of Afro-American Religion in the United States," History of Religions 2 (1971) 54-66.

670. Long, Norman G. "The Theology and Psychology of the Negroes' Religion Prior to 1860 as Shown Particularly in the Spirituals," M.A. thesis, 1936, Oberlin College.

671. McCarroll, Jesse C. "Black Influence on Southern White Protestant Church Music During Slavery," Ed.D. dissertation, 1972, Columbia University.

672. McGhee, Nancy B. "The Folk Sermon: A Facet of the Black Literary Heritage," College Language Association 13 (1969) 51-61.

673. McGready, James. "A Short Narrative of the Revival of Religion in Logan County," New York Missionary Magazine and Repository of Religious Intelligence 4 (Jan., Apr., May, June, 1803) n.p.

674. McKissick, Marvin Lea. "A Study of the Function of Music in the Major Religious Revivals in America Since 1875," M.M. thesis, 1957, Southern California.

675. Mays, Benjamin, E. The Negro's God: as Reflected in His Literature. Boston: Chapman and Grimes, 1938.

676. Mischel, Walter and Francis. "Psychological Aspects of Spirit Pocession," American Anthropologist 60 (1958) 49-60.

677. Mitchell, H.H. "Negro Worship and Universal Need," Christian Century 83 (1966) 396-398.

678. _____. Black Preaching. New York: J.B. Lippincott, 1970.

679. _____. "Black English," in Language, Communication, and Rhetoric in Black America Arthur L. Smith, ed. New York: Harper and Row, 1972, 87-100.

680. _____. Black Belief. New York: Harper and Row, 1975.

681. "Negro Prayer Meeting," American Missionary 36 (1882) 301.

682. Neher, Andrew. "A Physiological Explanation of Unusual Behavior in Ceremonies Involving Drums" Human Biology 34 (1962) 151-160.

683. Noreen, Robert G. "Ghetto Worship: A Study of the Names of Chicago Storefront Churches," Names 13 (1965) 19-38.

684. Onwreachi, Patrick. "Religious Concepts and Socio-Cultural Dynamics of Afro-American Religious Cults in St. Louis, Missouri," M.A. thesis, 1964, University of St. Louis.

685. Pearson, W.D. "Going Down to the Crossroads: The Blues-man and Religion," Jazz and Blues 2 (1972) 13-15.

686. "Pentecostalism on Black Campuses Growing, but Shepherds are Scarce," Howard University Sets Pace," Star-News (March 22, 1975) 41-45.

687. Pipes, William Harrison. "Old-time Negro Preaching," Ph.D. dissertation, 1943, University of Michigan.

688. _____. Say Amen, Brother! New York: William-Frederick Press, 1951.

689. Powdermaker, Hortense. After Freedom: A Cultural Study of the Deep South. New York: n.p. 1939.

690. Proctor, Henry H. "The Theology of the Songs of the Southern Slave," Southern Workman 36 (1907) 584-92.

691. _____. Between Black and White. Boston: Pilgrim Press, 1925.

692. Ray, Joseph E. "Black Ministers," African Missionary 36 (1992) 300-306.

693. Reid, Ira. "Let Us Pray!" Opportunity 4 (1926) 274-278.

694. Rice, John H. ed. "Attempts to Evangelize the Negro Slaves in Virginia and Carolina," Evangelical and Literary Magazine 4 (1821) n.p.

695. Rivers, Clarence Jos. Soulful Worship. Washington, D.C.: National Office for Black Catholics, 1974.

696. _____. "Toward Black Catholic Worship," Liturgy 20 (1975) 76-79.

697. _____. "Occular vs. Oral Culture: The Implications for Worship," Freeing the Spirit 5 (1977) 10-15.

698. Rosenberg, Bruce. The Art of the American Folk Preacher.
New York: Oxford University Press, 1970.

699. _____. "The Formulaic Quality of Spontaneous
Sermons," Journal of American Folklore 83 (1970) 335-350.

700. _____. "The Genre of the Folk Sermon," Genre
4 (1971) 189-211.

701. Ryder, Charles J. "The Theology of Plantation Songs,"
American Missionary 45 (1891) 123-124, 283; 46 (1892) 9-16.

702. Seale, L.M. "Easter Rock: A Louisiana Negro Ceremony,"
Journal American Folklore 55 (1942) 212.

703. Simpson, George E. "Black Pentecostalism in the United
States," Phylon 35 (1974) 203-211.

704. Snyder, Howard. "A Plantation Revival Service," Yale
Review (October, 1920) 169-180.

705. "Spirituals Churches; Sect Marks Fifty Years of Growth,"
Ebony (October, 1960) 69-70.

706. Spiro, Melford E. "Religious Systems as Culturally
Constituted Defense Mechanisms," Context and Meaning in
Cultural Anthropology. New York: The Free Press, 1965, 181-
211.

707. Steiner, R. "Seeking Jesus, a Religious Rite of Negroes
in Georgia," Journal American Folklore 14 (1901) 172.

708. Strong, James B. "Chicago Store Front Churches: 1964,"
Names 12 (1964) 127-128.

709. Sutton, Amos P. "What Happens on the Mourner's Bench,"
The Negro 5 (1947) 1-8.

710. Thurman, Howard. Deep River: Reflections on the Religious Insight of Certain Negro Spirituals New York: Harper.
1955.

711. Walker, Sheila S. Ceremonial Spirit Possession in Africa
and Afro-America. Leiden, Holland: E.J. Brill, 1972.

712. Walton, O.M. "A.M.E. Zion has Lively Sessions," Christian
Century 73 (1956) 732-733.

713. Washington, Joseph. Black Religion. The Negro and
Christianity in the U.S. Boston: Beacon Press, 1964.

714. _____. Black Sects and Cults. Garden City, N.Y.:
Doubleday and Co., Inc., 1972.

715. "Watch Meeting," Southern Workman 28 (1899) 151-155.

716. Williams, Charles H. "The Negro Church and Recreation," Southern Workman 55 (1926) 59-70.

717. Williams, Ethel and Clifton Brown, comps. Afro-American Religious Studies. Metuchen, New Jersey: Scarecrow Press, 1972.

718. Williams, Melvin D. Community in a Black Pentecostal Church: An Anthropological Study. Pittsburgh: University of Pittsburgh Press, 1974.

719. Williams, Robert Caroll. "A Study of Religious Language: Analysis/Interpretation of Selected Afro-American Spirituals, with Reference to Black Religious Philosophy," Ph.D. dissertation, 1975, Columbia University.

720. Williams, Robert Elbert. "The Negro Spiritual and Religious Symbolism," SM.M. thesis, 1950, Union Theological Seminary.

721. Wilson, Bryan. Religious Sects. New York: McGraw-Hill Book Co., 1970.

722. _____. The Noble Savages: The Primitive Origins of Charisma and Its Contemporary Survival. Los Angeles: University of California Press, 1975.

723. Winslow, David J. "Bishop E.E. Everett and Some Aspects of Occultism and Folk Religion in Negro Philadelphia," Keystone Folklore Quarterly 14 (1969) 59-80.

724. Woodson, Carter G. The History of the Negro Church. Washington, D.C.: The Associated Publishers, 1921.

725. Yinger, J. Milton and George E. Simpson. Racial and Cultural Minorities. New York: Macmillan, 1958.

6

Caribbean: Religion, Music, Culture, Folklore, and History

726. Abrahams, Roger. "Patterns of Performance in the British West Indies," in Afro-American Anthropology, Norman Whitten and John Szwed, eds. New York: The Free Press, 1970, 163-180.

727. _____. Deep the Water, Shallow the Shore: Three Essays on Shantying in the West Indies. Austin: University of Texas Press, 1974.

728. Bach, Marcus. Strange Altars. Indianapolis: Bobbs-Merrill, 1952.

729. Baez, Tony. "A History of Puerto Rican Protest Music: An Introduction," Canto Libre 1 (1974) 18-25.

730. Barrett, Leonard E. Soul Force: African Heritage in Afro-American Religion. New York: Doubleday Co., 1974.

731. _____. The Rastafarians. Boston: Beacon Press, 1977.

732. Bastide, Roger. African Civilizations in the New World. New York: Harper Torchbooks, 1971.

733. Baxter, Ivy. The Arts of an Island: the Develop of the Culture and of the Folk and Creative Arts in Jamaica, 1494-1962. Metuchen: Scarecrow, 1972.

734. Beckwith, Martha. Black Roadways: A Study of Jamaican Folklife. Chapel Hill: University of North Carolina, 1929.

735. Behague, Gerard. "Bossa and Bossas: Recent Changes in Brazilian Urban Popular Music," Ethnomusicology 17 (1973) 209-333.

736. _____. "Notes on Regional and National Trends
in Afro-Brazilian Cult Music," in Tradition and Renewal:
Essays on Twentieth-Century Latin American Literature and
Culture, Merlin Forster, ed. Urbana: North Illinois Press,
1975, 68-80.

737. Bolton, H. Carrington. "Gombay, a Festival Rite of
Bermudian Negroes," Journal American Folklore 3 (1890) 222-
226.

738. Bourguignon, Erika. "Ritual Dissociation and Possession
Belief in Caribbean Negro Religion," in Afro-American
Anthropology, Whitten and Szwed, eds. New York: The Free
Press, 1970, 87-102.

739. Bowers, Margaretta K. "Hypnotic Aspects of Haitian
Voodoo," International Journal of Clinical and Experimental
Hypnosis. No. 9 (1961) 269-282.

740. Bowes, Paul. "Calypso," The Negro 1 (1946) 66-68.

741. Braithwaite, Edward. The Folk Culture of the Slaves in
Jamaica. London: Villiers Publication Ltd., 1974.

742. Braithwaite, P.A. et al. Musical Traditions: Aspects of
National Elements with Influence on a Guyanese Community:
Vol. II. Georgetown: The Author, (187 Waterloo St.,), 1975.

743. Broadwood, L.E. "English Airs and Motifs in Jamaica,"
in Jamaican Song and Story, Walter Jekyll, ed. New York:
Dover, 1966, 285-288.

744. Brown, Wenzell. "Black Magic in the Virgin Islands,"
The Negro 4 (1946) 34-35.

745. Caldecott, Alfred. The Church in the West Indies.
London: Frank Cass and Co., Ltd. 1970.

746. Calley, Malcom. God's People: West Indian Pentacostal
Sects in England. London: Oxford University Press, 1965.

747. "Caribbean Music and Dance," Freedomways 4 (1964) 426-
434.

748. Carneiro, Edison. "The Structure of African Cults in
Bahia," Journal of American Folklore 53 (1940) 271-278.

749. Cassidy, Frederic. Jamaica Talk. London: Macmillan, 1961.

750. "Catholic Missionary Activity and the Negro Slave in
Haiti," Phylon 23 (1962) 278-285.

751. Courlander, Harold. Haiti Singing. Chapel Hill: University
of North Carolina Press, 1939.

752. Courlander, Harold and Remy Bastien. Religion and Poli-
tics in Haiti. Washington, D.C.: Institute of Cross-Cultural
Research, 1966.

753. Courlander, Harold. "Dance and Dance-Drama in Haiti,"
Function of Dance in Human Society, Franziska Boas, ed.
New York: Dance Horizons, 1972.

754. Creed, Ruth. "African Influence on Latin American
Music," M.M. thesis, 1947, Northwestern University.

755. Crowley, Daniel J. "Toward a Definition of Calypso,"
Ethnomusicology 3 (1959) 57-65; 117-124.

756. _____. "Song and Dance in St. Lucia,"
Ethnomusicology Newsletter 9 (1960) 4-14.

757. Cuney-Hare, Maud. "History and Song in the Virgin
Islands," Crisis 40 (1933) 83-93 ; 108, 118.

758. D'argent, Jacques. Voodoo. Los Angeles: Sherbourne Press,
1970.

759. Davis, Martha Ellen. "Afro-Dominican Religious Brother-
hoods: Structure Ritual and Music. Ph.D. dissertation 1976,
University Illinois at Urbana-Champaign.

760. Davis, Stephen. Reggae Bloodlines: In Search of the
Music and Culture of Jamaica. New York: Anchor Books, 1977.

761. De Jon, Lythe Ovure. "The Gombeys of Bermuda," Dance
Magazine 43 (1969) 32-33, 54-55.

762. Dolinger, J. "Land of the Walking Dead," Sepia
(November 1968) 17-75.

763. Douyon, Emerson. "Research Model on Trance and Possession
States in the Haitian Voodoo," A Paper, The Conference on
Research and Resources of Haiti, New York; November 1-9, 1967.

764. Dower, Catherine A. "The Afro-Caribbean Musical Legacy,
Part One: The Music of Puerto Rico," Musart 26 (1974) 52-56.

765. Dunham, Katherine. "The Dances of Haiti," n.p., 1938.

766. _____. Journey to Accompong. New York: Holt,
1946.

767. _____. "The Dances of Haiti," ACTA Anthropological 2 (1947) 5-61.

768. _____. Island Possessed. Garden City, New York:
Doubleday, 1969.

769. Dunnigan, A. "Haiti-Century of Christian Faith," Sepia
10 (1961).

770. Edwards, Charles L. Bahama Songs and Stories. Boston:
Houghton Mufflin and Co., 1895.

771. Elder, J.D. "Color, Music and Conflict: A Study of
Aggression in Trinidad with Reference to the Role of Traditional Music," Ethnomusicology 8 (1964) 128-136.

772. _____. "Morality in a Yoruba Ritual in Trinidad,"
in American Folklife, Don Yoder, ed. Austin: University Texas
Press, 1976, 64-88.

773. Espinet, Charles S. Land of the Calypso; the Origin and
Development of Trinidad's Folk Songs. Port-of-Spain, Trinidad:
Guardian Commerce Printery, 1944.

774. Epstein, Dena J. "African Music in British and French
American," Musical Quarterly 59 (1973) 61-65.

775. Frazier, E. Franklin. The Negro Family in Bahia, Brazil,"
American Sociological Review 7 (1942) 465-478.

776. Gaver, J.R. "Haiti, a Visit to Exotic Tropical Land of
Dreams," Sepia 11 (1962) 63-65.

777. Gonzalez-Wippler, Migene. Santeria: African Magic in
Latin America. New York: Doubleday Co., 1975.

778. Green, Barbara Joyce. "African Musical Survivals in the
Songs of the Negro in Haiti, Jamaica and the U.S." M.A. thesis,
1948, University of Chicago.

779. Green, Beryl A. "Folk Music in Jamaica B.W.I.," M.A.
thesis, 1951, Wayne State.

780. Griffin, Robert James, "Teaching Hispanic Folk Music
as a Means to Cross-Cultural Understanding," Ph.D. dissertation, 1973, Ohio State University.

781. Hadel, Richard E. "Carib Dance and Music," National
Studies (St. John's College, Belize City, British Hondures)
1 (1973) 4-10.

782. Handler, Jerome S. and Charlotte J. Frisbie. "Aspects of
Slave Life in Barbados: Music and Its Cultural Context,"
Caribbean Studies (1972) 5-46.

783. Hedrick, Basil C. and Jeanette E. Stephens. In the Days
of Yesterday and in the Days of Today: an Overview of
Bahamian Folk Music. Carbondale: University Museum, South
Illinois University, 1976.

784. Herskovits, Melville J. Surinam Folklore. New York:
Columbia University Press, 1936.

785. _____. "Drums and Drummers in Afro-Brazilian
Cult Life," Musical America 30 (1944) 477-492.

786. _____ . "The Social Organization of the Afro-Brazilian Candomble," Phylon 27 (1956) 83-101.

787. Herskovits, Melville J. and Frances S. Herskovits. Trinidad Village. New York: Octagon, 1964.

788. Herskovits, Melville J. "Some Economic Aspects of the Afrobahian Candomble," The New World Negro, Frances S. Herskovits, ed. Bloomington: Indiana University Press, 1966.

789. Hill, Errol. The Trinidad Carnival. Austin: University of Texas Press, 1972.

790. Hogg, Donald A. "Jamaican Religions: A Study in Variations," Ph.D. dissertation 1964, Yale.

791. Howard, Joseph. Drums in the Americas. New York: Oak Publications, 1967.

792. Hurston, Zora Neale. Tell My Horse. New York: J.B. Lippincott Co., 1938.

793. John Janheinz. "Blues and Calypso," Neo-African Literature: A History of Black Writing, Translated by Oliver Coburn and Ursula Lehrburger. New York: Grove, 1969, 166-182.

794. "Jamaica-Island Where Living is Easy," Sepia 10 (1961) 54-59.

795. "Jamaican Revivalist Cults," Social and Economic Studies 5 (1956) 321-442.

796. Jekyll, Walter. Jamaican Song and Story. New York: Dover Publication Inc., 1966.

797. Jones, Samuel B. "The British West Indian Negro: Customs, Manners, and Superstitions," Southern Workman 40 (1911) 580-589.

798. Kiev, Ari. "Folk Psychiatry in Haiti," Journal of Nervous and Mental Disorders 132 (1961) 160-165.

799. _____ . "Spirit Possession in Haiti," American Journal of Psychiatry 118 (1961) 133-138.

800. _____ . "The Therapeutic Value of Spirit-Possession in Haiti," Trance and Possession States, Raymond Prince, ed. Montreal: University of Montreal Press, 1968, 301-342.

801. Krugman, Lillian. Little Calypsos; Songs and Stories about West Indies. New York: C.V. Ray, 1955.

802. Lamson, Sophie Mollie. "Music and Culture in the Caribbean," M.A. thesis, 1957, Wesleyan University.

803. Landes, Ruth. "Fetish Worship in Brazil," Journal
American Folklore 53 (1940) 261-270.

804. Langguth, A.J. Macumba: White and Black Magic in Brazil.
New York: Harper and Row, 1975.

805. Lanternari, Vittorio. "Religious Movements in Jamaica,"
in Black Society in the New World, R. Frucht, ed. New York:
Random House, 1971, 308-312.

806. Leacock, Seth and Ruth. Spirits of the Deep. Garden City,
New York: Doubleday, 1972.

807. Lewin, Olive. "Folk Music of Jamaica: An Outline for
Classification," Jamaica Journal 4 (1970) 68-72.

808. _____. "Jamaica's Folk Music," Yearbook of the
International Folk Music Council 3 (1971) 15-21.

809. _____. Forty Folk Songs of Jamaica. Washington,
D.C.: General Secretariat of the Organization of American
States, 1973.

810. _____. "Biddy, Biddy: Folk Music of Jamaica,"
Music Educators Journal 63 (1976) 38-49.

811. Leyburn, James Graham. The Haitian People. New Haven:
Yale University Press, 1941.

812. Likes, Lisa. "The Origin and Development of Ethnic
Caribbean Dance and Music," Ph.D. dissertation, 1956, Florida
State University.

813. Lolderer, Richard A. Voodoo Fire in Haiti. Garden City:
Doubleday, 1935.

814. Lomax, Alan. "Haitian Journey," Southwest Review 23
(1938) 125-147.

815. Long, Joseph K. "Medical Anthropology, Dance and Trance
in Jamaica," Bulletin International Committee on Urgent
Anthropological and Ethnological Research (U.N.E.S.CO) no 14
(1972) n.p.

816. McBurnie, Beryl. "The Little Carib and West Indian
Dance," Caribbean Quarterly 14 (1968) 136-139.

817. McCloy, Shelby. The Negro in the French West Indies. New
York: Negro Universities Press, 1974.

818. McKay, Claude. Songs of Jamaica. Miami, Fla.: Mnemosyne
Pub., 1969.

819. Merriam, Alan P. "Songs of the Afro-Bahian Cults: an
Ethnomusicological Analysis," Ph.D. dissertation, 1951,
Northwestern University.

820. Merriam, Alan P., Sara Whinery and B.G. Fred. "Songs of a Rada Community in Trinidad," Anthropos 51 (1956) 157-174.

821. Metraux, R. "Some Aspects of Hierarchial Structure in Haiti," Acculturation in the Americas Sol Tax, ed. Chicago: University of Chicago Press, 1951, 264-278.

822. Midgett, Douglas K. "Performance Roles and Musical Change in a Caribbean Society," Ethnomusicology 21 (1977) 55-73.

823. Mintz, Sidney W. and Richard Price. An Anthropological Approach to the Afro-American Past: A Caribbean Perspective. Philadelphia: Institute for the Study of Human Issues, 1976.

824. Mischel, Frances.'"African 'Powers' in Trinidad: The Shango Cult," Anthropology Quarterly 30 (1957) 45-59.

825. Mischel, Walter and Frances. "Psychological Aspects of Spirit Possession," American Anthropologist 60 (1958) 249-260.

826. Moore, Joseph G. "Religion of Jamaican Negroes, A Study of Afro-American Acculturation," Ph.D. dissertation, 1953, Yale University.

827. _____. "Ritual Music and Dance in Cult Groups in Jamaica," Paper, IX International Congress of Anthropological and Enthnological Services, Chicago, 1973.

828. Myers, C.S. "Traces of African Melody in Jamaica," in Jamaica Song and Story, Walter Jeckyll, ed. New York: Dover Publications, 1966, 279-287.

829. Murray, Laura Bernice. "The Folk and Cult Music of Jamaica, B.W.I.," Ph.D. dissertation, 1971, Indiana University.

830. Nettleford, Rex. "The Dances as an Art Form-Its Place in the West Indies," Caribbean Quarterly 14 (1968) 127-135.

831. _____. Roots and Rhythms: Jamaica's National Dance Theatre. New York: Hill and Wang, 1970.

832. Newhall, Venetia. "Black Britian," Folklore 86 (1975) 25-41.

833. Norman, Alma. Ballads of Jamaica. London: Longmans, Green and Co., Ltd., 1967.

834. O'Gorman, Pamela. "The Introduction of Jamaican Music into the Established Churches," Jamaica Journal (Kingston) 9 (1975) 40-44, 47.

835. Parsons, E.C. "Spirituals and Other Folklore from the Bahamas," Journal of American Folklore 41 (1928) 467-524.

836. Pearse, Andrew. "Aspects of Change in Caribbean Folk Music," Journal of the International Folk Music Council 7 (1955) 29-36.

837. Pearson, Paul M. "Music in the Virgin Islands," Southern Workman 62 (1933) 454-456.

838. Pierson, Donald. "The Negro in Bahia, Brazil," American Sociological Review 4 (1939) 136-158.

839. "Rastafarians," Sepia 17 (1968) 72-75.

840. "Rev. Claudius Henry, Leader Rastafari Cult," Jet (November 17, 1960) 17.

841. Roberts, Helen H. "Some Drums and Drum Rhythms of Jamaica," Natural History 24 (1924) 241-251.

842. _____. "A Study of Folk-Song Variants Based on Field Work in Jamaica," Journal American Folklore 38 (1925) 149-157.

843. _____. "Possible Survivals of African Song in Jamaica," The Musical Quarterly 12 (1926) 340-358.

844. Rouff, Anthony E. "Authentic Facts on the Origin of the Steelband. St. Augustine, Trinidad: Bowen's Printery, 1972.

845. Ricks, George Robinson. "A Subjective Description of the Afro-Bahian Cults and their Music," M.M. thesis, 1949, Northwestern University.

846. Riqaud, Odette M. "The Feasting of the Gods in Haitian Voodoo," Primitive Man 19 (1946) 1-58.

847. Rummonds, F. "African Influence on Brazilian Folk Dancing," Viltis 25 (1966) 6-7.

848. Schmidt, Cynthia. "Shango Cult Music of Trinidad: The Annual Ceremony," M.A. thesis, 1974, University California, Los Angeles.

849. Schomburg, Arthur. "West Indian Composers and Musicians," Opportunity 4 (1926) 353-355, 363.

850. Shaw, Roberta Adeline. "The Possibilities for the Adaptations of Brazilian Folk Music to Protestant Worship," S.M.M. thesis, 1949, Union Theological Seminary.

851. Shedd, Margaret. "Carib Dance Patterns," Theatre Arts 17 (1933) 65-77.

852. Simpson, George. "The Shango Cult in Nigeria and in Trinidad," American Anthropologist 64 (1932) 103-134.

853. _____. "Vodun Service in Northern Haiti," American Anthropologist 42 (1940) 36-54.

854. _____. "Haiti's Social Structure," American Sociological Review 6 (1941) 640-646.

855. _____. "The Belief System of Haitian Vodun," American Anthropologist 47 (1945) 35-59.

856. _____. "Jamaican Cult Music," New York: Ethnic Folkways Library, 1954.

857. _____. "Magical Practices in Northern Haiti," Journal American Folklore 67 (1954) 395-403.

858. _____. "Political Cultism in West Kingston, Jamaica," Institute of Social and Economics Research Vol 4. Kingston: University of the West Indies, 1955.

859. _____. "Jamaican Revivalist Cults," Social and Economic Studies V. (1956) 334-336.

860. _____. "The Nine Night Ceremony in Jamaica," Journal American Folklore 70 (1957) 329-337.

861. _____. "Social Stratification in the Caribbean," Phylon 23 (1962) 29-46.

862. _____. "Baptismal, Mourning and Building Ceremonies of the Shouters in Trinidad," Journal American Folklore 79 (1966) 537-550.

863. _____. "Religious Cults of the Caribbean, Trinidad, Jamaica, and Haiti," Institute of Caribbean Studies, No. 7, Rio Piedras: University of Puerto Rico, 1970.

864. _____. Caribbean Papers. Centro Intercultural di Documentacion, 1970.

865. Smith, Ronald Richard. "The Society of Los Congos, of Panama: An Ethnomusicological Study of the Music and Dance-Theater of an Afro-Panamanian Group," Ph.D. dissertation, 1976, Indiana University.

866. Stevenson, Robert M. A Guide to Caribbean Music History: Bibliographic Supplement. Lima: Ediciones Cultura, 1975.

867. "Traditional Instruments Collection," Jamaica Journal 6 (1972) 52-53.

868. Waterman, Richard Alan. "African Patterns in Trinidad Negro Music," Ph.D. dissertation, 1943, Northwestern University.

869. Welch, David. "West African Cult Music Retentions in Haitian Urban Vandou: A Preliminary Report," Essays for a Humanist. Spring Valley, New York: Town House Press, 1977, 337-349.

870. Williams, Eric. Negro in the Caribbean. New York: Haskell House, 1971.

871. Williams, L. "Black Gold of Jamaica," Melody Maker 47 (1972) 32-38.

872. Wynter, Sylvia. "Jonkonnu in Jamaica: Toward the Interpretation of Folk Dance as a Cultural Process," Jamaica Journal 4 (1970) 34-48.

873. "That New Black Magic," Sepia 17 (1968) 62-67.

Catalogue of the Compositions of Afro-American Gospel Composers (1938-1965)

7

Identifying Printed Black Gospels

It is impossible to establish an irrefutable method of distinguishing printed Black gospels from printed White gospel songs; there are, however, some features of printed Black gospels that are unique. To make this distinction, the following "signals" have been established and are helpful if the composer of a gospel is unknown to the researcher, especially since some gospels are known only by title: (1) sheet-music cover format; (2) compositional style; (3) dedication; (4) title; (5) name of the author, composer, or arranger; and (6) publishing house.

Sheet-Music Cover Format

This is the most obvious feature of Black gospel music. Regardless of the publishing house, the format of the cover is generally the same. The title of the song is printed in bold inch-high type; cover decorations are kept at a minimum, usually consisting of a series of parallel vertical lines an inch from the left margin. Figure 1 illustrates the cover of a gospel song. The sheet music of lesser-known composers often includes a photograph of the composer on the cover. In several instances, the photograph is useful in establishing the race of the composer. However, because the photographs are generally of poor quality, this distinction cannot always be made. The covers of White gospels, on the other hand, are for the most part decorated with sketches of flowers, people, and objects that reflect the theme of the text or title.

Compositional Style

The publishers and arrangers, recognizing the desire for improvisation and individual interpretation, as well as the low level of academic musical training

Figure 1. Title page of "Rock My Soul"

of their public, write the music as simply as possible. One Black gospel music publisher composer explained the reason for the simplified arrangements:

> We don't write it too difficult by including all the harmony. The people who play it [gospel music] are not interested in harmony. There is no attempt to include perfect cadences and the like. It's not written for trained musicians . . . [it is] written for second graders so to speak. A musician is a slave to notes. It's not written for that kind of person. It's written for a person who can get the melody and words and interpret the song for himself. We [the arrangers] give only the basic idea and the person suits his own concept. If it were written correctly, we would go out of business. They wouldn't buy it . . . too complicated.[1]

Figure 2 is an arrangement of "Rock My Soul" to illustrate the point that these songs are written so that the person with little or no formal music training can read the score. Since many who play for Black churches and Black choirs read music with some difficulty, the compositional styles are practical.

The desire for simplified arrangements results in a preponderance of fundamental chords: tonic, subdominant, and dominant chords. One writer views the use of fundamental chords in repeated though inverted positions as monotonous:

> The exclusive use of the tonic, subdominant and dominant chords is repeated throughout several adjoining measures with little change in inversions, the results are monotonous.[2]

The writer, however, feels that the concepts conveyed in the term *monotonous* are ethnocentric. Repetitious rhythmic ideas are desired and part of the gospel aesthetic. Even though tonic harmony may be written, for example, for three measures, what occurs in actual performance in terms of rhythmic complexities and voicings is certainly not monotonous. Variety is achieved through the use of various rhythmic motives, and not through chordal progressions. Emphasis is on voice interplay in actual performance. Printed Black gospel songs use the lead-chorus format almost exclusively. The interaction between the chorus and leader phrases forms a strict short-phrase overlapping call-and-response pattern, and the harmonic phrases sung by the chorus tend to have strong melodic individuality in addition to rhythmic and harmonic interest. Figure 3 clearly shows that the chorus supports the solo voice or the lead; the chorus generally establishes a rhythmic motif that is constant throughout the song. Rhythmic motivic repetition does not always dictate word repetition. The use of rhythmic motives in response patterns is characteristic of printed Black gospels. Finally, the use of chords in first and second inversions in a series in the treble clef is an ubiquitous style of arrangement in printed black gospels (Figure 4).

ROCK MY SOUL

Arr. by
Roberta Martin

by
JAMES CLEVELAND

Figure 2. Score Portion of "Rock My Soul"

The   storms   of   life   are   rag - ing   high   Some -
My   en - i - mies   won't   let   me   be   And
Old   sa - tan's mad   and   I   am   glad   He

times   I   laugh,   some - times   I   cry,   Some -
why   they   talk   I   can - not   see   I
missed   this   soul   He   thought he   had   I

times   I   smile,   Some - times   I   frown,   Some -
go   my   way   and   do   no   wrong   That's
know   just   what   He's   grum - bling   'bout   He's

times   I'm   le - vel   to   the   ground.__
why   I'm   sing - ing   zi - on's   song.__
chained   in   hell   and   can't   come   out.__

ROCK MY SOUL · 2

Jesus Is the Answer
HE'S ALL I NEED

A Roberta Martin Arrangement

By WILLIE WEBB

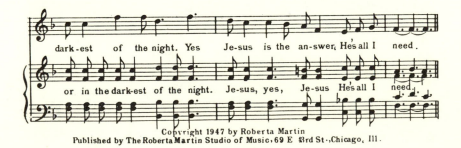

Figure 3. Score Portion of "He's All I Need"

VERSES

1. I'm a pil - grim, a stran - ger, I'm seek - ing that home that the
2. There is noth - ing so pre - cious as Je - sus to me ev - en
3. Tho the storms of this life may my path - way be - tide I am

He's all I need, He's all I need, He's all I need, He's all I need,

Lord pre - pared for me, for me, All to
more than I e'er dreamed could be What a
hap - py for I know my guide Let the

He's all I need, He's all I need, Je - sus is all I need

Him I've sur - ren - dered, and now ____ I see that
won - der - ful thing, I'm a child of the King praise
storm bil - lows roll Je - sus keeps . My soul I'll

He's all I need, He's all I need, He's all I need, He's all I need,

Je - sus is ____ All that I need ____
God He is All that I need ____
trust Him He is All that I need ____

Yes, Je - sus is all, All that I need ____

All That I Need -2

GOD IS STILL ON THE THRONE

Dedicated to my friend Mrs. Clara Blanks

Arr. by
Roberta Martin

by
ROBERTA MARTIN

Figure 4. Score Portion of "God Is Still on the Throne"

CHORUS

God is still on the throne with - in your

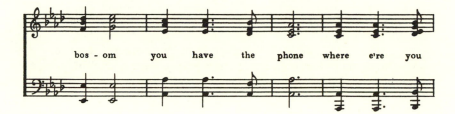

bos - om you have the phone where e're you

walk you're not walk - ing a - lone __ re - mem-ber

God __ is still on the throne __

God is Still on the Throne - 2

Dedication

The Black gospel songs that this writer examined generally included dedications; the practice is so widespread that only a few Black gospel songs are published without them. Gospels are dedicated to individuals and performing groups. Dedications often refer to the individual's church, church position, and the city in which the individual resides. The dedication appears in small italicized type under the inside title of the song, just above the score.

Often the occasion for the writing of a gospel is given on the page facing score:

> The title, words, and music of this song was composed by Estelle V. McKinley Banks a native of Atlanta, Georgia. During the rendition under the influence of the Holy Spirit that great host of witnesses expressed themselves joyously and without reserve. This song is a gift to me from the Holy Spirit.[3]

or

> Dr. W. H. Brewster is the foremost gospel songwriter minister in America today. His songs are distinguished by their specific historical background and technical scriptual indoctrinal value. Too many songs are afloat that represent only rhythmical and sentimental value. Every gospel song should set forth some doctrine or redemptive proposition of the New Testament Church. These qualities are evident in all of Dr. Brewster's songs. His scholarly background and rich experience through years of distinguished service as one of the nation's most effective radio and pulpit personalities are all contributing factors to his matchless gift as a songwriter. His songs will live.[4]

In addition to the dedication that appears under the song's title, credit is sometimes given to the singer or group that popularized a particular song. For example: "I Can't Forget It Can You" *as sung by* the Gospel Chorus Antioch Baptist Church, Chicago, Illinois, or "Hold Me (Please Don't Let Me Go)" *as sung by* Mahalia Jackson.

Title

Stock phrases or phrases that are familiar to a gospel audience from prayers, testimonies, scriptural paraphrases, and congregational utterances and preaching often become the title of gospels or formulae in gospel texts. This writer has heard the following gospel titles (selected randomly from the catalogue) used formulaeically or as stock phrases in testimonies, prayers, sermons, and in some cases hymns, spirituals, and other gospels:

"He Is My All and All"
(John Carney Bagby)

"He's My King"
(Ruth Davis)

"Christ is the Answer"
(Eugene Hamilton)

"Jesus is a Rock"
(Myrtle Jackson)

"Oh Lord, Oh Lord"
(Samuel Allan Lewis)

"Lord Remember Me"
(Dorothy Norwood)

"Come On Jesus"
(Dorothy Norwood)

"Sword and Shield"
(L. J. Reese, Jr.)

"I Feel the Holy Spirit"
(Clara Ward)

"We're Going to Have A Time"
(Clara Ward)

The very frequent reference to Jesus Christ in titles of gospels is an aspect of Black gospels that cannot go unnoticed. One explanation for this is offered by James Cone, who explains Christology: "Statements about God are not theologically distinct from statements about Jesus Christ."[5] Although Cone refers to the spirituals, his comments are applicable to gospels, since gospel songs often reflect the same kind of existential tension that is expressed in the spirituals. Cone goes on to add that "Jesus is understood as the King, the deliverer of humanity from unjust suffering. He is the comforter in time of trouble, 'the lily of the valley', and 'the bright and morning star.'"[6]

Gospel titles often convey a personal involvement with Jesus:

"He Delivered Me"
"Searching for a Friend"
"He is my All and All"
"Depending on Jesus"
"Have You Got Jesus"

The word choice *Lord, He, Jesus,* and *Friend* in referring to Jesus often depends largely upon the rhythm of the language in which people express their desire to be free (liberated), rather than upon the intellectual content of the language.[7] Many of the gospel titles are personal testimonies, often of the writer's "trials and tribulations" and how Jesus "brought them through":

"He Delivered Me"
"Jesus Supplies Your Every Need"
"Conversation with Jesus"
"I'm Going to Tell How His Love Lifted Me"

Gospel titles and texts deal with the immediate problems affecting Blacks and are specifically designed to help Black people to surmount immediate circumstances of their lives. These titles unequivocally reveal an unshakeable faith of a community of believers in a world full of trouble.

Name of the Author, Composer, or Arranger

There are certain first names and first-name combinations that are traditionally used by Black people. For example, such names as Beulah, Sechrist, Everlenia, Eldoris, Darsilla, Lula, Willie Lou, Cassietta, Mae Dell, Ella Mae, and Magnolia are in the repertoire of Black names.

Publishing House

During gospel's peak—the forties and fifties—there were approximately six major gospel publishing companies in existence. The following publishers and publishing companies published the bulk of gospel music: Thomas A. Dorsey (who has now sold out to Hill and Range), Martin and Morris, The Roberta Martin Studio of Gospel Music, Sylvia Bodder Music Studio, Thurston Frazier, Bowles Music House, Venice, Theodore Frye, Emma and Carl's, Good Shepherd Music House, First Church of Deliverance, and Andrea, to name the larger publishers.

These six signals—the sheet-music cover format, compositional style, dedication, title, name of the author, composer, or arranger, and publishing house—are useful to those researchers who are unfamiliar with the printed Black gospel music repertoire.

Notes

1. George Robinson Ricks, *Some Aspects of the Religious Music of the U.S. Negro: An Ethnomusicological Study with Special Emphasis on the Gospel Tradition* (Ph.D. dissertation, Northwestern University, 1960), p. 143.

2. Katherine Lucille Small, *The Influence of the Gospel Song on the Negro Church* (M.A. thesis, Ohio State University, 1945), p. 34.

3. "I Am the Battlefield for My Lord," Viola McKinley, 1948. Composed by Viola McKinley.

4. "Surely Our God Is Able," Bowles, 1950. Words and music by Herbert Brewster.

5. James Cone, *The Spirituals and the Blues* (New York: Seabury Press, 1972), p. 47.

6. Ibid.

7. Ibid.

8

Organization of Black Gospel Music

It seems worthwhile to provide some background information on how gospels have been classified and catalogued by the Library of Congress.

All gospels are routinely classified in Class M, which is "Vocal Church Music." Class M is further divided in the following way:

M2146. Detached hymns, etc. (Generally tear-sheets of some hymn to be included in a collection).
M2198. Temperance, revival, rescue, mission, gospel, etc., song collections (sacred and secular).
M2199. Temperance, revival, rescue, mission, gospel, etc., songs (sacred and secular), single items.

The original classification schedule provided for further division of classes M2198 and M2199 by using subsidiary letters and numbers referred to as "cuttering."[1] Unfortunately, classification schemes are subject to personal interpretation, and the classifiers did not keep to the details of the scheme.[2]

Before 1940 Black gospel music was classified routinely in M2146 because the first copyrighted gospels were similar in appearance to the tear-sheet hymns, which were classified in M2146 or the "detached hymns" class. Sometime during the late 1940s, Black gospel music was classified in M2199 rather than in M2146. In effect, M2146 and M2199 became equivalent classes; M2146 was limited to material copyrighted before 1940 and M2199 to material copyrighted after 1940.[3]

M2198 is the class for collections of gospel songs. Generally these collections amount to small gospel songbooks that usually contain a large number of old, standard gospels but sometimes include new songs. A publisher would submit for copyright the few new items in the collection rather than the entire collection or book. M2198 contains few Black gospel songbooks because the publishers of black gospel songs depend on the individual publication of the songs for copyright protection.

The card catalogue for class M2199 is complete up to 1970; however, the boxes of music are complete to about 1965. Since 1965 there has been no effort to file single-sheet music items.

It should be further pointed out that single-sheet music items (gospel songs both Black and White) are arranged according to the classification schedule; there is no attempt made to alphabetize by author or composer these single-sheet items.

Notes

1. U. S. Library of Congress Processing Department, Subject Catalogue Division, *Classification: Class M Music and Books on Music,* 2d. edition (Washington, D.C.: Library of Congress, 1917 [revised 1968]).

2. Interview, Wayne Shirley, Librarian, Music Division, Library of Congress, June 1972.

3. Ibid.

9

Key to the Catalogue

Entry Information:

Name of Composer (birthdate*)

Title of Gospel, Arranger,* Publishing Company,*
  City or Address of Publishing Company,*
  Copyright year

Abbreviations Used:

Arrangers

JT:	Jeanette Tall
KW:	Kenneth Woods, Jr.
KM:	Kenneth Morris
RM:	Roberta Martin
TD:	Thomas Dorsey
TF:	Theodore Frye
TFz:	Thurston Frazier
VD:	Virginia Davis

Publishers

AC:	Alma and Carl's, Detroit
An:	Andrea Music, New York
CW:	Clara Ward Publishing House, Philadelphia
GS:	Good Shepherd Music House, Gary, Indiana
HR:	Hill and Range Songs, Inc., Beverly Hills
LB:	Bowles Publishing House, Chicago
LC:	Lucie Campbell Music Publishers, Memphis
MM:	Martin and Morris, Chicago
RM:	Roberta Martin Studio, Chicago
SA:	Simmon-Aikers Music House, Los Angeles
TD:	Thomas Dorsey, Chicago
TF:	Theodore Frye Music, Chicago
Ve:	Venice Music, Inc., Hollywood

*where available

Aaronson, Lazarus Andres (1903)

    God Didn't Curse Me When He Made Me Black, 1951

    I Saw Though My Eyes Were Closed, 1950

Adams, Wallace D. (1902)

    I'm Working For My Saviour, Margarite Brown, MM, 1947

    Let Me Live In This World In Jesus Name, MB, MM, 1948

    Lord, I'm Willing, LB, 1953

    Tell Jesus When He Comes, MM, 1952

    There Is Room In Heaven For You, MB, MM, 1947

    This Is A Long Journey To Travel, MM, 1947

    Trust In Jesus He's All Right, Surriah Robinson, MM, 1957

    You Have A Race You Must Run Someday, MB, MM, 1948

Aikens, Margarite

    A Brighter Day Ahead, KW, MM, 1956

    God's Healing Water, Esma Williams, 1957

    Thy Grace Is Sufficient For Me, EW, 1957

    I Cannot Tell, EW, 1957

    Is There Room, EW, 1957

    Jesus All Around Me, EW, 1957

    Safe Within The Fold, EW, 1957

Aikers, Doris Mae (1922)

    Deeper In The Lord, Manna Music, 1958

    Don't Stop Using Me, Manna Music, 1958

    God Is So Good, TFz, 1956

    God Will If You Will, 1958

    Grow Closer, TFz, 1952

    He Delivered Me, SA, 1948

Aikers, Doris Mae

    He Knows And He Cares, TFz, Manna Music, 1958

    He's A Light Onto My Pathway And Lamp Unto My Feet,
       Gwendolyn Cooper, SA, 1957

    He's Alright With Me

    He's Everywhere, 1954

    I Never Knew Joy Before, Charles J. Levy, 1949

    I Want A Double Portion of God's Love, KM, MM

    I Want To Go Deeper In The Lord, TFz, 1955

    I Was There When The Spirit Came, KM, 1954

    It Means A Lot To Know Jesus For Yourself, Don Lee White,
       1951

    I Found Something, Maxine Blackburn

    Jesus Is Born Today

    Keep The Fire Burning In Me, KW, MM, 1947

    Lead Me, Guide Me, 1953

    Lead On, 1955

    Life Eternal, Charles J. Levy, 1955

    Look At The Cross Again, 1955

    Look At The Hill, Don Lee White, SA, 1952

    Mine Just For The Asking, Manna Music, 1958

    My Expectation, Charles Levy, 1951

    A Servant For Thee, 1955

    The Smile On His Face Never Fades, Manna Music, 1958

    Trouble, Manna Music, 1958

    You Can't Beat God Giving, Manna Music, 1957

Alexander, Clearance

    Child of God, Well Done, VD, LB, 1949

    The Lord Has Been Good To Me, 1950

Alexander, Clearance

    Close To Thee, KM, 1956

    Hold On, MM, 1956

    Jesus Knows, KM, Ve, 1955

    Lord Help Me Carry On, KM, Ve, 1953

    Jesus I'm Thankful, KM, Ve, 1951

    Jesus Is The First Line of Defense, KM, Ve, 1951

    Jesus Met The Women At The Well, KM, MM, 1949

    Peace Of Mind, KM, Ve, 1951

Alexander, James W.

    Bless Us Today, KM, Ve, 1956

Allan, George N.

    Must Jesus Bear The Cross, John Walter Davis and Dotie
        Mae Norris, Chicago, 1946

Allen, Eleanor F. (1920)

    Hallelujah, My Work Is Done, KM, 1952

Allen, Luschaa

    The Dawning Of The Day, 1949

Alwood, J.K.

    The Uncloudy Day, KM, 1957

Anderson, Robert,

    God Knows The Reason Why, 1954

    I Know Prayer Changes Things, VD, GS, 1947

    My Posession Word, Charles Levy Gary, GS, 1955

    Nothing Shall Disturb My Faith, VD, 1954

    Oh, Lord Is It I, VD, 1953

Anderson, Viola Isabelle

   Jesus Is All I Need, Dorothy Bade, 1957

Andrews, Letha Marie (1911)

   When The Gold Touches The Gray, 1955

Androzzo, Alma Irene (1912)

   Deliver Me From Evil, KM, 1950

   Doing Good Deeds, VD, LB, 1951

   He's Such A Great Saviour, RM, 1951

   I Am Willing Lord To Walk With Thee, VD, LB

   I Carry My Burdens To The Lord And Leave Them There, RM
      1951

   I Will Walk With Jesus, KM, 1952

   If I Can Help Somebody, KM, 1948

   I'll Live For Jesus Twenty-Four Hours A Day, VD, LB, 1951

   I'll Make It Somehow, revised KM, 1950

   I'll Tell About Him, Choral, VD, LB

   I Have Something To Tell About Jesus, VD, 1951

   Jesus Is All The Friend I Need, W.O. Hoyle, LB, 1952

   The Way Of The Cross Leads Home, VD, LB, 1951

   What He's Done For Me, VD, LB, 1952

   Live In The Sunlight, Boosey Hawkes, 1964

Armstead, Juanita

   I Can Feel The Fire Burning In My Soul, KW, 1956

Armstrong, Evylyn Irene (1925)

   Let's Keep Our Eyes On Jesus

   What About Yours, 1952

Armstrong, Margarite

    I'm Glad I Heard Him Whisper In My Heart, music Celeste
        Scott, VD, LB, 1951

Austin, David L.

    Fly Away, KW, LB, 1963

    For This I'm Thankful, 1962

    He Did It, 1962

    Jesus Is The Answer, 1962

    O Lord Send Your Child, 1962

Austin, Dorothy (1916)

    My Journey To The Sky, Austin Studio of Gospel Music,
        639 N. 46th St., Philadelphia, Pa., 1944

    Say Yes To The Will Of God, words Lillian Maddox, KM, 1952

Austin, James

    Soldier Of The Cross, RM, 1969, (Ded: Roberta Martin
        Austin)

Austin, William

    Kneel Down At The Altar, RM, 1958

Bagby, Harry Carney

    Glory, Glory, Glory To The New Born King, An

Bagby, John (Carney)

    He Is My All And All, An

Baldwin, Mrs. L.P. (1905)

    If Jesus Had To Pray What About Me, MM, 1941

Ballou, Rev. Thomas L.

    Lord, Let Me Cling To Thee, W.H. Miller, pbc, 16 E. 18th
        Ave., Gary Ind., 1945

Banks, Ann (1912)

   Searching For A Friend, VD, RM, 1952

Banks, Estelle (1898)

   Let Down Your Sword And Shield, 1948

   Let Jesus Help You He Understands, 1947

   Working Out My Soul Salvation, 1948

   I Am On The Battlefield For My Lord, TD, 1943

   We Walk Together My Lord And I

   Lay Down Your Sword And Shield, pbc, 1949

   Let Jesus Help You Understand, pbc

   There'll Be A Happy Time In Heaven One Of These Days, 1947

Banks, Mable

   I Am The One, Alice A. Fields, pbc, 1944

   Who Wouldn't Serve A God Like Thee, pbc, 1944

Banks, Mary Johnson

   Then Jesus Came, 1961

Banks, Martha Eason

   A Christian's Prayer, choral KM, 1954

   Lord, Touch Me, Clare Ward, 1955 (Rec: Ward Singers)

Banks, Ross

   I Thank God For All He's Done For Me, special arr. KM,
       MM, 1949

Barber, Keith

   I've Got A Mother Gone Home, KM, Ve, 1951 (Rec: Pilgrim
       Travelers)

Bartell, Beuhal Sechrist

   My Wonderful Lord, pbc, 1958

Bates, James M.

   They Crucified My Saviour, He Arose, KM, LB, 1936

Bates, Viola

   Trust In Jesus, 1944

Battle, Bernard Gary (1916)

   I'm Going To Sing Hallelujah By And By, Mary E. Lacy
      Moore, Battle and Odum, Washington, D.C., 1947

   I Want To See His Face Some Sweet Day, Alyce Fields, 1944

   Just Hold On, MLM, MM, 1944

   Sunlight From Heaven (Shining On My Soul), Ray Forrest,
      1944

Baynes, Caudye

   Depending On Jesus, Mary E. Lacy Moore, 1966

Beale, Beatrice

   Great Day, KM, MM, 1951

   Great Day When We All Gather Home, Harold Smith, MM,
      1958, (Operatic gospel Anthem)

   I'm Held By His Hand, KM, 1956, (Ded: First Church of
      Deliverance)

   It Will Be A Great Day, MM, 1951

   Jesus Can Do Anything For You, KM, MM, 1953

   When I Whisper To God In Prayer, special arr. KM, MM,
      1954

Beall, V.B.

   Lift Him Up, KM, MM, 1959, (Feat: Original Gospel Har-
      monettes)

Beattie, Ruth (1920)

    In Jesus' Name, H. Holmes, Carroll Music Studio, 650 Gates
        Ave., N.Y., 1953

Belcher, Reginald

    Tell The Love Of Jesus

Bell, Coretha (1927)

    Answer Me, KM, MM, 1955

    He's Coming Back For Me, VD, Robert Anderson, Jr., GS,
        1954

Bell, Jewellm (1911)

    I'm Going To Fight For The Right Until I Die, KM, 1955

Bell, Maude E. (1918)

    Be Thou Faithful, R.L. McKenney, pbc, Buffalo, N.Y., 1947

    I Know The Lord Will Go With You All The Way, R.L.
        McKenney, pbc, 1956

    Lord, I'm Trying, Is My Way Alright?, 1947

    You Ought To Have Been There When The Blessed Saviour
        Died, A.P. Windon, 1953

Bell, Wilbur John

    Are You Traveling On The Right Road, Watkins Music Studio,
        Newark, N.J., 1943

    I Need Jesus (To Carry Me Through), Watkins Studio, 1950

    I'll Tell It, Tell It, Tell It, Watkins Studio, 1949

    I've Got To Tell You (What The Saviour Has Done For Me),
        Watkins Studio, 1952

    Joy, Joy, Joy, Watkins Studio, 1943

    Let It Be Known, Weary Traveler, Watkins Studio, 1943

Benford, Thomas (1925)

    He's By Your Side, Freddie Harris, St. Louis, Mo.

    Have You Got Jesus

    Jesus Will Show Me The Way

Bennett, Kathleen

    Wait On The Lord, KW, Music Mart, Indianapolis, Ind., 1956

Berry, Darsella

    I Say A Prayer Every Night, Blair's, 1906 Clemet St.,
       Detroit, Mich., 1961

Betts, Nathaniel (1921)

    I Can't Serve The Lord As I Desire, Aletha Robinson,
       Hatcher Music House, Brooklyn, N.Y.

    I'm Going To Rest From My Labor Afterwhile, 1948

    There's Only Room Enough For Jesus In My Heart, Aletha
       Robinson, 1948

Biddix, Viola Baker

    I Was Aware When The Change Came, 1946

    So Sayeth The Lord, 1944

Boddie, Sylvia

    Meeting On The Old Campground, Sylvia Boddie Music Studio,
       Chicago, Ill., 1948

    Now Lord, JT, 1948

    Someday I'll Hear My Jesus Call My Name, JT, 1948

    Just Let Him In, JT, 1948

Boissiere, Mildred (1897)

    Jesus The Healer, 1952

Boland, Clay

    Pray, General Music Publishers, N.Y. (Feat: Delta Rhythm
        Boys)

    Trust In Him, Amber Music, 1957

Bolden, Alfred

    The Great Commandments, Ralph Goodpasteur, First Church
        of Deliverance, Chicago, Ill., 1964

    I'll Praise His Name, AC, 1963

    Jesus Will Bring Things Out Alright, words James Cleveland,
        TFz, Frazier and Cleveland, 1962

Bonner, Eldoris

    Leave Your Nets, 1959

Bowles, Lillian M.

    Don't Take Everybody To Be Your Friend, words W.P.
        Anderson, KM, LB, 1939

    God's Going To Separate The Wheat From The Tare Didn't
        He Say, Didn't He Say, KM, 1939

    Here I Am Lord, Send Me, W.O. Hoyle, LB, 1937

    He's Everything To Me, KM, 1938

    I Promised The Lord That I Would Hold Out, Willie Webb,
        KM, 1938

    I Want Jesus To Walk Around Me, words Five Soulstirrers,
        KM, LB, 1939

    Walk Around, Walk Around, Walk Around With Jesus

    I'm Tramping Trying To Make Heaven My Home, KM, 1939

    Twelve Gates To The City, TF, W.O. Hoyle, LB, (Rec:
        Tuskegee Four Quartet)

Boyce, Everlenia

    Jesus Is The Keeper Of My Soul, V. Dickens, Chicago, Ill.

    This Is That Spoken By The Prophet Joel, KW, LB, 1961

Boyd, Jeanetta M.

   The King's Highway, KM, pbc, 1962

Boyer, James

   Going Back To My God, KM, MM, 1954, (Rec: Boyer Brothers)

   I Can Feel God's Power, KM, MM, 1954

   Walk Together Children, KM, 1954

   When Life Is Done, KM, MM, 1954

Bradford, Alex Prof.

   After It's All Over, RM, 1963

   At The End, RM (words, music), 1953

   Blessed Mother, La Bostrie, KM, Ve, dist. by MM, 1965,
      (Bessie Griffin Consoleters)

   Come On In The Room, RM, HR and RM, 1952

   Do You Know Jesus, RM, 1953, (Barbara Troy South Park
      Baptist Church)

   Glorious Glory, KM, 1951

   Go Forth In The Name Of The Lord, choral arr. KM, 1958
      (Sung by Cobb)

   God Is Good To Me, KM, 1952, (Gladys Banks, Bradford
      Singers)

   God Never Sent A Soldier To Battle Alone, KM, 1960

   He Is Such An Understanding God, KM, 1961

   He Lifted Me, KM, Ve, 1954 (Recorded Specialty)

   He Makes All My Decisions For Me, KM, 1959

   He Will Deliver Our Souls From Sin, RM, 1953

   He'll Be There, RM, 1952

   He's A Light In Darkness, RM, 1962, (Rec: South Park
      Baptist Church)

   He's A Wonder, KM, 1952

   He's Everything To Me, KM, 1958, (Rec: Bradford Singers)

Bradford, Alex Prof. (continued)

Holy Ghost, KM, 1965

I Can't Tarry, KM, Ve, 1956

I Don't Care What The World May Do, KM, Ve, 1963

I Feel The Spirit, KM, Ve, 1954

I Heard Him When He Called My Name, RM, 1953, (Rec:
    Roberta Martin Singers)

I Know He Lives In Me, United Record, LB, 1952

I Want To Ride That Glory Train, KM, 1960

I Won't Sell Out, KM, Ve, 1954

No, No I Won't Sell Out

I'm Too Close To Heaven To Turn Around, RM, 1953, (Rec:
    Roberta Martin Singers)

I'm Tramping Trying To Make Heaven My Home, KM

In Him I Found Perfect Peace, KM, 1953

Is My Name On The Roll, KM, 1962

It All Belongs To Him, KM, 1958

I've Got A Job, KM, 1958

Let Us Praise The Lord, KM, 1953

Lo, Is The Way, RM, 1952 (Rec: Roberta Martin Singers)

I've Got To See Jesus, One Of These Mornings, KM, 1951

Jesus Is A Friend Until The End, KM, MM, 1952

Just The Name Jesus, KM, Ve, 1954

Leak In The Building, KM, 1960

Let God Abide, RM, 1952

Let Us Praise The Lord, KM, 1953

Life's Candlelight, KM, Ve, 1955

The Lord Jesus Is My All And All, KM

Lord, Lord, Lord, KM, Ve, 1954

Bradford, Alex Prof. (continued)

    Lo, Is The Way, 1952, (Rec: Roberta Martin Singers)

    My Crown, KM, 1953

    My Reward Is In Heaven, KM, 1953

    O Lord, Save Me, KM, Ve, 1955

    On My Way Home, KM, 1953

    Right Now, KM, Ve, 1954

    Said I Wasn't Going To Tell Nobody, KM, 1960

    Since I Met Jesus, RM, 1953

    Someone, RM, 1956

    Steal Away, Ve, 1957

    Sweet Jesus,KM , HR , 1961

    Ten Thousand Blessings, KM, 1959

    Thy Word, KM, 1953

    Turn Away From Sin, KM, 1953

    We're Marching To The City Of God, RM, 1953

    What Did John Do, KM, 1958

    When Jesus Comes, KM, 1957

    Who Can I Blame, KM, 1953

    Without A God, Ve, 1956

    You Can't Make Me Doubt Him, MM, Pathway House of Music,
       N.Y., 1963

Bradford, Richard

    Jesus Will Hear You Pray, RM, 1958

Bradley, Clyde

    Keep In Touch With Jesus, KW, LB, 1963, (Rec: Sallie
       Martin Singers)

Bradley, J.R.

    Joy, Joy, Joy In Living For The Lord, TF, W.O. Hoyle, LB, 1941

Brazier, Ethel Lee (1921)

    Worthy Is The Lamb Who Died To Set Us Free, words Asiah King, TFz, MM, 1947

Brewster, Herbert Clay (1900)

    I Thank You Lord, RM, 1945

Brewster, W. Herbert Rev.

    The Lord Gave Me Wings, VD, LB, 1952

    Make Room For Jesus In Your Life, W.O. Hoyle, LB, 1947 Brewster Ensemble)

    More Of Jesus And Less Of Me, VD, LB, 1951, (Brewster Ensemble)

    Move On Up A Little Higher, W.O. Hoyle, LB, 1946, (Ward Singers)

    One Morning Soon I Heard The Angels Singing, VD, LB, 1950

    Only The Crumbs, Berrford Shephard, 1954

    Our God Is Able, VD, TF, W. Herbert Brewster, 1949

Brewster, W.H., Jr. and Sr.

    Out On The Hill, VD, TF, 1952

    Peace Be Still, VD, 1949, (Brewster-Aires)

    Scatter Sweet Roses Along Life's Way, LB, 1953, (Feat: Ward Singers)

    Sometime, Somewhere, Someday, Somehow, W.O. Hoyle, LB, W. Herbert Brewster, 1953

    Speak To Me Jesus, W.O. Hoyle, LB, 1947

    Surely God Is Able, VD, TF, W.H.B., 1950, (Ward Singers)

    That's Enough For Me, VD, TF, WHB, 1952

Brewster, W.H., Jr. and Sr. (continued)

These Are They, VD, 1949

Treading The Wine Press Alone, Ward, Brewster, 1955, (Ward Singers)

Whatever Else I Need, VD, LB, W.H.B., 1949

When We Walk Through The Water, VD, 1952

Within Those Jasper Walls, W.O.H., LB, 1953

The Wonderful Counselor Is Pleading For Me, Ward

At The End Of The Road, VD, TF, WHB, 1952

Can You Tell Anything He Has Done For You, VD, Josephine Daniels, 1946

God's Amazing Love, Ward, 1954 (Ward Singers)

Have Faith In God, VD, TF, 1952

He Died In Calvery, WOH, LB, 1947

He Has A Way That Is Might Sweet, VD, TF, WHB, 1949

He'll Fix It All, VD, LB, 1950

He'll Make It All Clear At Last, WOH, LB, 1947

The Hope Of The World Is Jesus, VD, TF, WHB, 1949

How Far Am I From Canaan?, KM, MM, 1946

How Long, O Lord, How Long?, Ward, W.H.B., 1953 (Rec: Ward Singers)

I'm Holding On, VD, TF, 1952

I Found The Keys Of The Kingdom, VD, LB, 1952

I Just Can't Afford To Fail My Jesus Now, VD, Josephine Daniels, TF, 1946

I Know It Was Jesus, VD, WHB, LB, 1952

I Know The Time And The Place, VD, Josephine Davis, TF, 1946

I Thank You Lord, Q.C. Anderson, RM, 1945

I Want The Lord To Smile On Me, VD, WHB, LB, 1949

I Want To Get Closer To The Lord, VD, 1949

Brewster, W.H., Jr. and Sr. (continued)

 I Will Kneel Down At The Cross, VD, 1959

 I Will Wait On The Lord, WOH, WHB, LB, 1947

 I'll Be There, VD, 1946

 I'll Never Forget How My Jesus Brought Me Through, WOH, LB, 1947

 I'm Climbing Higher and Higher, Ward, WHB, LB, 1954 (Rec: Ward Singers)

 I'm Getting Nearer To My Home, VD, LB, 1949

 I Am Still On The Glory Road, VD, TF, 1949

 Just Over The Hill, VD, 1949

 Jesus Is All, VD, LB, 1949

 Jesus Knows And Will Supply My Every Need, WOH, 1947

 Jesus The Perfect Answer, VD, TF, 1949

Bridges, Charles and Lillian Bowles

 When I Get Home, VD, LB, 1942, (Birmingham Jubilee Singers)

Broadnax, William

 Calvery, KM, MM, 1951, (Spirits of Memphis Quartet)

Brooks, Anne C. Grahm (1913)

 Do You Know Who Jesus Is, Brooks Mucis Studio, 1951

 Family Prayer

 He'll Never Let Go My Hand, Brooks Music Studio, 1951, (Angelic Gospel Singers)

 Holy Night

 I'm Glad He's Right On Time, Brooks Music Studio, 1951

 Only Four Gospels In The Book (Bible), 1951

 When I Get Inside, 1957

Brooks, Elder

   Until I Found The Lord, RM, 1939

Brougher, Goldie Wade

   A Wondrous Friend, VD, LB, 1952

Brown, Rev. A.D.

   Don't Wait Too Late To Save Your Soul, Margarite Brown,
      Jackson Studio of Music, 4311 So. Mich. Ave., Chicago,
      Ill., 1947

Brown, Andres

   I Found Him, R. Lee McKinney, Buffalo, N.Y., 1969

Brown, Beatrice

   God Is Everything To Me, J.T. Highbaugh, Jr., Brown's
      Music House, Indianapolis, Ind., 1958

   God Is Near, KW, 1958

   God Is Your All, KW, 1957

   He Will Answer Prayer, KW, 1956

   I Need Your Lord, KW, 1961

   I Want To Walk In The Footprints Of The Lord, 1965

   Jesus Is Real To Me, KW, 1963

   Look And Live, KW, 1957

   Without God I Could Do Nothing, KW, 1959, (Rec: Raymond
      Rasberry Singers)

   Yes Lord Let Thy Will Be Done, KM, 1960

Brown, Faye Ernestine (1918)

   I Am Happy In The Service Of The Lord, VD, MM, 1945

Brown, Lula Phillips (1904)

   God Is A-Searching, Margarite Brown, MM, 1950

Brown, Marie P.

    I'm Going To Tell God Just How You Treat Me, Dorothy
       Pearson, pbc, 1966

Brown, Mylan G., Jr.

    Do You Know What Jesus Means To You, KM, 1954

    Just Jesus, KW, 1950

Brown, Rosa Lee (1921)

    By The Grace Of God I've Come A Long Way, RM, 1949

Brown, Samuel Elzie (1890)

    He's Wonderful, pbc, 1947

    I Let My Jesus In

Burgess, Rev. Bobby

    I've God Something To Shout About, KW, First House of
       Prayer, Chicago, Ill., 1965

Burgis, William E.

    Come On Over, VD, LB, 1952

Butler, Dorothy W.

    Faith In The Power Of God, Lily Welch, Brown Music House

    Faith In The Power Of God, Lily Welch, 1021 Congress Ave.,
       Indianapolis, Ind.

    The Way No Other One Can Do, KM, Brown Music House, 1962

Butler, Effie

    Blessed Are They, W.O. Hoyle, LB, 1952

    Let Him In, 1953

    Step Out On God's Word, 1953

Butler, John

    Our Bread Of Life, James Hendrix, Emma Carl, Detroit,
       Mich., 1963

Butts, Magnolia Lewis

    Breath On Me, W.O. Hoyle, TF, LB, RM, 1945

Byars, Fredella

    Everyday, KM, 1963

Cadenao

    Rock Me To Sleep, KM

Caesar, Shirley

    Carry Me Home, KM, 1959

Cain, Sherman Fletcher

    Down On My Knees, Manna Music, 1951

Caldwell, O.

    Thanks Be To God, VD, 1962

Campbell, Charles E.

    Have No Fear For Jesus Is Near, KM, 1953

    I Waited For The Lord To Save My Soul, KM, 1955

    Lord If You Try Me Again I Won't Fall, KM, 1956

Campbell, Lucy E.

    Even A Child Can Open The Gate, 1952

    Footprints Of Jesus, 1949

    God's Long Reach And Salvation, 1958

    He Understands, He'll Say Well Done, 1950

    Heavenly Sunshine, 1951

Campbell, Lucy E. (continued)

   His Grace Is Sufficient For Me

   I Need Thee Precious Lord

   In The Upper Room With Jesus, 1952

   Jesus Gave Me Water, 1950

   Just As I Am, 1951

   Just To Behold His Face, 1951

   Looking To Jesus, 1950

   Love And Not Nails Held Him There, 1961

   My Lord And I, 1951

   Not Yours But You, 1951

   The Path Through The Valley Leads Home, 1958

   A Sinner Like Me, 1952

   Something Within, 1950

   The Story Of Salvation Must Be Told, 1961

   David Wait Upon The Lord, 1952

   Touch Me Lord, Jesus, 1950

   Unto Thee Thy Holy One, 1961

   When I Get Home, 1950

Carr, Mary Lee

   Beyond This Veil Of Sorrow

   I Have A Date With Jesus Christ My Lord, 1950

   Jesus Is All (My Hope And Stay), 1952

   O My Lord What A Day, 1950

   What Evil Has This Man Done, Carr's Music Studio, 343 E.
      101 St., N.Y., 1952

   Yes There's A God Who Cares For Me, 1952

   You Can Look For Me In Heaven (I'll Be There), 1950

Carr, Wynona (1924)

    The Ballgame, KM, Ve, 1953

    Conversation With Jesus, MM, Ve, 1952

    Did He Die In Vain?, MM, Ve, 1952

    Don't Miss That Train, MM, Ve, 1950

    Going Home, MM, Ve, 1956

    That Good Ole Way, MM, Ve, 1951

    He'll Be Waiting At The End For Me, MM, Ve, 1950, (Rec: Brother Joe May)

    He's Able To Carry You Through, MM, Ve, 1951, (Rec: Brother Joe May)

    I Heard Mother Pray One Day, MM, Ve, 1953

    I Know By Faith, MM, Ve, 1953

    I Know Someday God's Going To Call Me, MM, Ve, 1951

    I See Jesus, MM, Ve, 1951, (Rec: Brother Joe May)

    I'll Serve You Lord Until My Dying Day, MM, Ve, 1950

    In A Little While, MM, Ve, 1952

    It's Alright, MM, Ve, 1951

    A Letter To Heaven, MM, Ve, 1953

    O Yes He Set Me Free, MM, Ve, 1951 (Rec: Brother Joe May)

    On The Other Side, MM, Ve, 1952

    Our Father, MM, Ve, 1951

    See His Blessed Face, MM, Ve, 1953

    What Do You Know About Jesus, MM, Ve, 1950

    What You Gonna Do When You Get To Heaven, MM, Ve, 1951

Clarke, Mattie Moss

    Climbing Up The Mountain, Herbert Pichard, AC, 1965

    He's The Answer He's The One

    Hold Me Jesus In Thy Hand

Clarke, Mattie Moss (continued)

   I Thank You Lord, AC, 1963

   I'll Never Turn Back No More, 1962

   Jesus Supplies Your Every Need, 1966

   Lead Me On, 1966

   None But The Pure In Heart, 1964

   Nothing Comes Between Me (And My Saviour), 1964

   Sanctify Me Holy, 1964

   Saved Hallelujah, Emma Carl's, 1962

   Wonderful, Wonderful, 1962

   Wonderful, Wonderful, Yes He Is, 1963

Clark, Sylvia

   Teach Me To Pray, RM, 1965 (Sung: Roberta Martin)

Cleveland, James

   Grace Is Sufficient, RM, 1958, 1959, 1960

   Ain't That Good News, 1959

   Beyond The Dark Clouds

   Caste All Your Cares On Him, RM, 1960

   Christ Is The Answer, TFz, 1962

   Come Into My Heart, Lord Jesus, RM, 1954

   Come, Lord Jesus, RM, 1962

   Count Your Blessings, KM, 1952

   Down In My Heart, KM, 1962

   Every Now And Then, RM, 1956

   Give God The Credit, KM, 1960

   God Is A Good God, KM, 1962

   Good Enough For Me, KM

Cleveland, James (continued)

    Had It Not Been For Him, KW, 1960

    Have You Ever Seen A Man Like Jesus, KM, 1955

    He Cares For Me, KM, (Rec: Caravans)

    He Comes To See About Me, RM, 1959

    He's Got His Eyes On Me, KM, 1960

    He Never Forgets His Own, KM, 1955

    He Won't Fail, RM, 1960

    He'll Fill Every Space In Your Life, KM, 1952

    He'll Make You Happy, RM, 1956

    He'll Work A Wonder, RM, 1956

    He's Alright With Me, KM, 1960, (James Cleveland Allstars)

    He's Done Something For Me, RM, 1961

    He's Everything You Need (Come Rain Or Shine), RM

    He's Got Everything You Need, TFz, 1962

    He's Leading Me, RM

    He's Real (Twenty-Four Hours Of The Day), KM

    He's So Good, TFz, 1963

    He's Using Me, RM, 1955

    His Name Is Worthy, KM, 1961

    Hold Me Jesus, RM, 1959

    I Gave My All To The Lord, KM, 1959 (Rec: Caravans)

    I've Just Got To Make It, RM, 1964

    I Never Knew (Such Joy Before), KM, 1956

    I Shall Know Him (In The Sweet By And By), RM, 1962

    I Stood On The Banks Of The Jordan, KM, 1967

    I Want To See Jesus, Myrtle Scott's Studio of Gospel
        Music, 3113 Giles Ave., Chicago, Ill., 1950

    If You Want To See The Lord, KM, 1954

Cleveland, James (continued)

    I'll Keep On Holding To His Hand, RM, 1961

    I'm Climbing, RM, 1955

    I'm Determined, RM

    I'm His Child, RM, 1961

    I'm In Christ, RM, 1956

    I'm Still Saying Yes To The Lord, Jeanette Sims, KM, 1953

    It Keeps Me Happy All Day, KM

    It Was The Blood, RM, 1961

    It's Going To Rain, RM, 1959

    I've Got A New Born Soul Since The Holy Ghost Took Control, RM, 1954

    Jesus Lifted Me, RM, 1954

    Jesus' Love Bubbles Over (In My Heart), RM, 1962

    Jesus Will, KM

    Jesus Like He Said Would, KM

    Keep Looking Up, RM, 1954

    King Jesus How I Love Him, RM, 1954

    Listen The Lambs A-Crying, RM, 1954

    Look Up And Live, RM, 1961

    The Lord Is Standing Up (On The Inside Of Me), KM, 1955

    The Lord Will Provide, KM, 1958

    Malachi 3:10 (Try Jesus), KM, 1960

    My Job Is Working For Jesus, KM, 1959

    My Lord Is Watching You, KW, 1961

    My Soul Looks Back And Wonders, How I Got Over, Ve, 1959

    No Trouble At The Water, KM, (Rec: Caravans)

    Nothing But A God, RM, 1955

    O Glory I'll Fly Away, RM, 1954

Cleveland, James (continued)

    O How I Love Jesus, KM, 1960 (Rec: Caravans)

    O How Much He Cares For Me, RM, 1960

    O Lord I Surrender To Thee, KM, 1955 (Rec: Sallie Martin)

    O Lord Stand By Me, RM, 1952, (Rec: Brother Joe May)

    One More River To Cross, KM, 1955, (Rec: Soulstirrers)

    One Step At A Time, KW, LB, 1960

    Redeemed, TFz, 1962

    Rock My Soul, RM, 1958

    Saved, RM, 1955

    Sell-Out (To The Master Right Now), KM, 1954

    Someday I'm Going To Put On My Golden Shoes, KM, 1958

    Since I Met Him, RM, 1960

    Take Me To The Water, KM, 1956

    Take Them And Leave Them There, KM, 1964

    Talk To Jesus, RM, 1954

    That's Just Like The Lord, KM, 1961

    That's What A God Is For, KM, 1956, (Rec: Mahalia Jackson)

    That's What He's Done For Me, TFz, 1962

    There's A Man (On The Other Side Of Jordan), RM, 1965

    Trouble In My Way, RM, 1955

    Trying To Make A Hundred, RM, 1955

    Until My Jesus Comes, 1955

    Walk In Jerusalem, (new version) RM, 1957

    Walk On By Faith, RM, 1962

    While I Have A Chance, KW, Manna Music, 1954

    Why Do I Love Thee, 1958

    There's No Condemnation, KM, 1958

Cobbs, Rev. Clarence H.

Christ Won't Fail, First Church of Deliverance, Chicago,
Ill., 1961

Cockrell, Emmanuel M.

Bless This Church And Bless Our Church

Bless This Revival

Glory, Glory To God

God Is On His Throne and Not Dead

God's Love Is Free

Put All Of My Faith In God

Just As Soon As I Reach My Home, 1965

Let The World See Jesus In You, 1963

Lord Teach Me, 1965

Teach Me, 1965

Peace Is So Sweet, 1965

Coleman, Henrietta

Don't Forget That You Live In The Presence Of The King,
Coleman's Studio of Gospel Music, Cleveland, Ohio

I Just Can't Tell You How I Felt, KM, 1964

O Yes I'm Waiting On The Lord, Helen Turner, 1949

There Is A Place On The Battlefield For Me, HT

Well Let's Talk About Jesus, KM, 1946

Conner, Evangelist M.A.

The Gospel Shoes, pbc, Chicago, Ill., 1956

Cook, Lucille Mack

Lord Have Mercy On Your Children If You Please, Margarite
Brown, Manna Music, 1948

Cook, Sam

    Be With Me Jesus, KM, Ve, 1960 (Soulstirrers)

    He's Been A Shelter For Me, KM

    Just Another Day, KM, Ve

    Nearer To Thee, Ve, (Soulstirrers)

    Stand By Me Father

    Touch The Hem Of His Garment

Cook, Walter

    I Am Sealed, RM, 1949

Cosby, Abe

    Stand The Storm, KM, 1957

Cowans, Mother Minnie Elizabeth

    Well Done, W.H. Taylor, 1953

Craig, Rev. Charles

    Blessed Jesus Hold My Hand, First Church of Deliverance
      1964

    I Trust In You, Ralph Goodpasteur, 1962

    Passing My Saviour, 1963

    We've Come A Mighty Long Way, RG, 1963

Crain, Roy

    He's Welcome Me (To My Home), KM, Ve, 1953 (Soulstirrers)

    It Won't Be Very Long, KM, Ve, 1952, (Soulstirrers)

    I'm So Glad, KM, Ve, 1955

    Jesus I'll Never Forget, RM, Ve, 1954 (Soulstirrers)

Crawford, Lucillia Wilson

    Calvery's Hill, pbc Cincinnati, Ohio, 1961

Crawford, Percy

    I Found A Friend, VD, Staff Publ. Co., Chicago, Ill., 1960

Crawford, Vernon

    Wait Upon The Lord, Fred Martin, cop. Vernon, Crawford, 1961

Crocker, Ruby Sims

    Insurance With Jesus, Ruby Sims Co., Pa., 1951

    O, I Believe, 1951

    After A While It Will All Be Over

    Christ Is Real, 1947

    Let Jesus Fix It For You, 1947

Crosby, Drexsella J.

    God Will Reward You In The End, 1957

Crume, Leroy

    The Love Of God, KM, Ve, 1958

Davis, Mary J.

    God Knows All About Me, RM, 1944

    Have You Any Witness In Your Heart, RM, 1944

Davis, Ruth

    He's Here Right Now, 1959

    He's Mine, 1957

    He's My King, 1957

    Jesus Gently Can Guide Me, 1957

    Jonah, 1959, (Rec: Davis Sisters)

    My Wonderful Counselor, 1958

    Not A Word, 1960

Davis, Ruth

Oh Sinner, 1957

Rain In Jerusalem, Clara Ward, 1956

Save Me, KM, 1960

There's A Tree On Each Side Of The River, CW, 1957

This Is My Prayer, MM, 1958

We Need Power, KM, Plane Mar Music Co., 1959

Wouldn't It Be Wonderful Over There, KM, 1957

Davis Sisters

Farewell, KM, 1958

Get Right With God, KM, 1957

Davis, Virginia

All Through The Night, TF, 1950

The Battle Will Be Over Afterwhile, LB, 1943

Behold That Star, LB, 1950

Do You Know Jesus Saves The Soul?, TF, 1951

Fit Me For Service, Lord I Pray, LB, 1942

Have You Tried My Blessed Saviour, He's Alright

He'll Answer Pray, TF, 1950

He's So Wonderful, TF, 1947

I'm Waiting On The Lord, 1946

I Am Walking In The Sweet Holy Way, LB, 1951

I Call Him Jesus My Rock, 1950, (Ded: Rev. L. Boddie)

I Called On The Lord And Got An Answer, First Church of
    Deliverance, 1950

I Have A Friend Above All Others, TF, 1946

I Heard His Voice One Day

I Thank You For Your Goodness, TF, 1949

Davis, Virginia (continued)

I'll Just Go On Serving Jesus, LB, 1942

I'm Going To Glory Land, VD

I'm Going To Tell How His Love Lifted Me, TF, 1945

I'm So Glad I Heard His Voice, LB, 1950

I'm Trying To Make It Home To Glory, LB, 1951

In Answer To Prayer, LB, 1950

It's Much Later Than You Think, 1950

I've Got To Keep On Praying, LB, 1951

Jesus Is Risen, LB, 1944

Jesus Lives In My Soul, TF, 1948

Jesus My Lord Is In Command

Jesus The Light Of The World

Let Jesus Fix It, Carter's Music House, Memphis, Tenn.,
    LB, 1943

My God's Going To Get Tired Afterwhile, 1947

My Mother Bowed And Prayed For Me, TF, 1949, (Sung:
    Pilgrim Travelers)

Never A Word Did He Say, 1943

Oh Lord Forgive, Palestine Peters, Carrolsburg Place,
    Washington, D.C., 1945

Please Show Me The Way, LB, 1951

Precious Things Desired, PP

Saviour Walk With Me, VD, TF, VD Anderson Music Co., 1961

Take, Eat, This Is My Body, LB, 1943

Tell God All About It, LB, 1951

That Living Water Will Cleanse Your Soul, LB, 1951

There Is Nothing Impossible With God, 1963

There Will Be Peace In Heaven, LB, 1943

This Is My Prayer, LB, 1951

Davis, Virginia (continued)

    A Wandering Sheep In God's Hands, LB, 1961

    The Water From Heaven Will Cleanse Your Soul, TF, 1950

    What A Friend We Have In Jesus, LB, 1943

    When I Touch The Hem Of His Garment, TF, 1950

    Yes My Lord I Know I Got Religion, LB, 1940

Dickens, Viola Bates

    By And By I'll See Jesus, Dickens, 1440 W. 14th St.
       Chicago, Ill., 1955

    Hallelujah, Jesus Saves, Bates, 1942

    In Jesus There's Rest For The Weary, pbc, 1953

    Jesus I Can't Live Without You, pbc, 1953

    Let Jesus In, Ryan and Dickens Studio, Warren Blvd.,
       Chicago, Ill., 1962

    You'll My All, Ryan and Dickens Studio, 1962

    Master Teach Me The Way, RD, 1965

    Nobody But Jesus, pbc, 1955

Diggs, Cora Francis

    Remember Me O Lord I Pray, pbc, 1154 19th St., N.Y.

    Someday Soon He'll Make It Plain, pbc, 1953

    Telephone To Glory, pbc

Dinwiddie, Julia E.

    Jesus The Answer To Your Prayer, KM, 1947

Dixon, Jessye

    The Failure's Not In God, RM, 1964

    God Can Do Anything But Fail, KM, 1959

    The Hope Of This World Is Jesus, RM, 1964

Dixon, Jessye (continued)

   I Thank You Lord You've Certainly Been Good To Me, RM

   Jesus Will See You Through, MM, 1961, (Sung: James
      Cleveland)

   Since His Love Came Into My Heart, KM, 1961

   There Is No Failure In God, RM, 1962

Dixon, Naomi Hedgewood

   I've Got Jesus On My Side, William Petty, 1952

Dennis, Archie

   Thank You Lord For Sparing Me, KW, GS, 1958

   When He Calls My Name, RM, 1965, (Sung: Roberta Martin
      Singers)

Darden, Madame Ruby

   Jesus He'll Be There, Gospel Music Studio, 619 N. 38th
      St., Philadelphia, Pa., 1952

Dourhety, Nina

   I Know The Lord Has Been With Me, Each Step Of The Way,
      Dorothy Pearson, LB, 1953

David, Prew

   Lord Come By Here, 1960, (Sung: North Philadelphia Juniors)

   Use Me Lord, KM, 1960

Davis, Alfreda

   Father I'm Coming Home, KM, 1961, (Sung: Davis Sisters)

Davis, James

   He's Going To Carry Me Home, VD, LB, 1953

Dent, Hugh

    Come Now, Hugh Dent Studio of Church Music, 1407 Lawrence
        Ave. E. St. Louis, Ill.

    Glory In The Cross, 1950

    Have Faith In God, RM, KM, 1957

    I Abide In His Love, MM, 1953

    I Am Centered On His Love, HD, 1951

    I'm Getting More Like Jesus Everyday, TD

    I'm Going To Stand Up

    In That Day, Windon, 1950

    Jesus Lives, Windon, 1949

    When I Finish My Work, KM, 1955

Derricks, Clevant

    God's Got His Eyes On You, LB, 1943

    Hail The King, LB, 1938

    Hallelujah, Praise His Name, 1937

    He's Going To Make The Way Easy By and By, LB, 1942

    Lord, Don't Forsake Me, 1943

    Mothers Of Heaven, LB, 1942

    My Soul Is Satisfied, 1943

    Oh Lord Stand By Me, 1943

    Remember Me, LB, 1943

    When God Dips His Love In My Heart, 1940

    When He Blessed My Soul, 1937

    Where The Love Of God Came Down, 1944

    Yes I'm Newborn Again, 1938

Dorsey, Thomas A. (All entries that follow are pbc unless
                   otherwise indicated)

An Angel Spoke To Me Last Night, 1953

He's All I Need, 1949

He Never Will Leave Me, 1949

He Is The Same Today, 1933

God Is Good To Me, 1943

God Be With You, 1940

Forgive My Sins, Forget And Make Me Whole, 1938

Everyday Will Be Sunday, 1957

Don't Forget The Name Of The Lord, 1950

Do You Know About Jesus, 1933

Did You Ever Say To Yourself That I Love Jesus, 1962

Diamonds From The Crown Of The Lord, 1953

Consideration, 1953

Come Unto Me, 1946

Behold A Man Of Galilee, TD and Louise Shropshire, 1957

Be Thou With Me All The Way, 1943

Angels Keep Watching Over Me, 1954

I'm Going To Walk Right In And Make Myself At Home, 1938

I'm Going To Work Until The Day Is Done, 1951

I'm Going To Wait Until My Change Shall Come, 1944

I'm Climbing Up The Rough Side Of The Mountain, 1952

I'll Never Turn Back, 1944, (Feat: Clara Ward)

I'll Be Waiting For You At The Beautiful Gate, 1955

If You See My Saviour, 1929

If We Never Needed The Lord Before, We Sure Need Him Now,
   1943

I Want Two Wings To Veil My Face, 1952

Dorsey, Thomas A. (continued)

    It's Not A Shame To Cry Holy To The Lord, 1946

    I Thought On My Way, 1952

    I May Never Pass This Way Again, 1947

    I Know Jesus, 1935

    I Got Heaven In My View, 1933

    I Don't Know What You Think of Jesus, 1941

    How Much More Of Life's Burden Can We Bear, 1947

    I Can't Forget It, Can You?, 1933

    Hold On A Little While Longer, 1945

    Hold Me (Please Don't Let Me Go), 1958

    Hide Me Jesus In The Solid Rock, F.E. Mason, TA, 1939

    Hide Me In Thy Bosom, 1939

    He's All I Need, 1944

    I'm Going To Walk Right In And Make Myself At Home, 1938

    I'm Just A Sinner Saved By Grace, 1937

    I'm Satisfied With Jesus In My Heart, 1934

    I'm Singing Everyday, 1934, (Ded: Gospel Singers of
       America)

    I'm Waiting For Jesus, He's Waiting For Me, 1945

    In My Saviour's Care, 1953

    It Don't Cost Very Much, 1954

    Jesus Rose Again, 1950

    Jesus Remembers When Others Forget, 1941

    Jesus Only, 1950

    Jesus Never Does A Thing That's Wrong, 1936, (Sung:
       Thomas Dorsey singers)

    Jesus Lives In Me, 1937

    It's All In The Plan Of Salvation, 1934

Dorsey, Thomas A. (continued)

It's A Highway To Heaven (Walking Up The King's Highway),
    Mary Gardner and TD, 1954

It Is Real With Me, 1934

Just One Step, 1950

Just Look Around, HR, 1952

The Day Is Past And Gone, HR, 1952

Old Ship Of Zion, 1950, (Sung: Norsalus McKissick and
    Roberta Martin)

The Savior Is Born, 1950

Never Leave Me Alone, 1951

The Lord Will Make A Way Somehow, 1943

Look, Look, Look Lord Down Upon Me, 1944, (Sung: Wilson
    Jubilee Singers)

You Can't Go Through This World By Yourself, 1933

Won't You Come And Go Along, 1941

When I've Sung My Last Song, 1943

When Day Is Done, 1947

What Could I Do If It Wasn't For The Lord, 1944

Trouble About My Soul, 1933

Oh Lord Show Me The Way, 1934

Singing In My Soul, 1932

Somebody's Knocking At Your Door, (Sung: Hamilton Singers)

Somewhere, 1947

Surely My Jesus Must Be True, 1933

Take Me Lord Take Me Through Lord, 1944, (Sung: Gertrude
    Ward and Daughters)

Maybe It's You And Then Maybe It's Me, (Sung: Radio Choir,
    First Church of Deliverance)

Lord Look Down Upon Me, 1944, (Sung: Etta Jennings, Ruth
    Sloane)

Dorsey, Thomas A. (continued)

    The Lord Will Make A Way Somehow, 1943 (Sung: Wilson
        Jubilee Singers)

    The Little Wooden Church On The Hill, 1949, (Ded: Memory
        of the old country churches attended by forefathers)

    Life Can Be Be Beautiful, 1940 (Sung: James Roberts)

    Let Me Understand, 1949, (Sung: Hatcher Temple Singers)

    A Man Who Loves Music Should Be One Who Loves Devotedly
        Whether It Be His Country, His Family, His Home, Or
        His God, 1946

    My Soul Feels Better Right Now, 1951

    Never Leave Me Alone, 1951

    Oh Ship Of Zion, (Sung: Norsalus McKissic and Roberta
        Martin Singers)

    The Savior Is Born, 1950

    Search Me Lord, (Ded: Brooklyn Westchester Choral Union
        and Associated Unions)

    Singing Everywhere, 1960

    Someday, Somewhere, 1941

    Someway, Somehow, Sometime, Somewhere, 1951

    Something Has Happened To Me, 1954

    Some Day I'll Be At Rest, 1956

    Some Day I'm Going To See My Jesus, 1941 (Sung: W.D. Cook
        Gospel Choir)

    Tell Jesus Everything, 1949, (Sung: Choir, Second Baptist
        Church of L.A., California)

    This Man Jesus, 1949

    Thank You All The Days Of My Life, 1946

    That's Good News, 1949

    There's A Better Day Coming Right Now, 1936

    Walk Over God's Heaven

    Want To Go To Heaven When I Die, 1959, (Sung: Bates Singers)

Dorsey, Thomas A. (continued)

    We Must Work Together, 1960

    What The Good Lord's Done For Me, (Sung: Brother Joe May)

    When They Crown Him Lord Of Lord, 1951, (Sung: Dorsey
        Celestrial Gospel Trio)

    While He's Passing By, 1964

    Windows Of Heaven, 1955

    You've Got To Right Each Wrong Day, 1934

    Your Sins Will Find You Out, 1946

    Let Every Day Be Christmas, HR, 1956

    Let The Savior Bless Your Soul Right Now, 1955

    Take My Hand Precious Lord, 1938

Dotson, Love W.

    Cry Unto The Lord, LB, 1958

    Lord Give Me The Strength To Help Others, O. Steward Wilson,
        LB, 1958

Douroux, Margaret J.

    Give Me A Clean Heart, Rev. Earl A. Pleasant, MT. Moriah
        Baptist Church, 470 W. 43rd St., L.A., Calif.

Downing, Lula Jones

    Victory Is Our Eternal Song

Drake, Esther

    Lord I Need You, RM, Martin Studio, 1964

Dupree, John A.

    The Jordan Happiness, RM, Martin Studio, 1966

Durham, Rev. M.C.

    Climbing Up High Mountains, Bowles and Morris, LB, 1939

    Jesus Will Win, VD, LB, 1943

Edson, Louis

    How Tedious And Tasteless, KW, LB, 1963, (Feat: and Rec:
       Eugene Burke, Sally Martin Singers)

Edwards, Johnny M.

    I'm Living For God, words Annie M. Edwards, AME, 1946

Edwards, Verdell McGee

    I Know Jesus, He's A Mighty Good Friend, J.T. Hidebaugh,
       Jr., Hidebaugh, Cleveland, Ohio, 1950, (Sung:
       Choraleer Gospel Singers, Ohio)

Epps, Willie Louise

    Jesus Whispered A Prayer To Me, Mary Lacy Moore, LB,
       1953, (Ded: Ward Singers)

    You Better Decide Which Way, W.L. Epps, LB, 1952

Esters, Helen B.

    I Will Follow Jesus, H.B. Esters, 1947

    Oh For A Heart To Serve Jesus, pbc, 1947

    Won't You Pray, pbc, 1947

Evans, Annell

    He Fixed It Long Ago, KM, MM, 1955

Evans, Carter

    I Know We'll Have A Time, First Church of Deliverance

    I Am Glad I Know Jesus Down In My Heart, Ralph Goodpasteur,
       FCD, 1956

Evans, Clay

By And By, pbc, 1947, (Feat: Lux Singers)

Jesus Knows, Margarite Brown, pbc, 1950

Run To The Lord, KW, Fellowship Baptist Church, Chicago,
    Illinois, 1961

Show Me The Way, KW, FBC, 1957

Soon Lord, MB, pbc, 1950

Evans, Georgia Ella Williams

God Will Be Your Friend, KM, MM, 1954

Famous Blue Jay Singers, Birmingham Alabama

Jesus' Love Is Just Flowing Over In My Soul, pbc, 3609
    Cottage Grove Ave., Chicago, Ill., 1947

There's No More Crying, pbc, 1947

Five Soulstirrers, Houston, Texas

He's My Rock, My Sword, My Shield, KM, 1938

Farmer, Rev. Miss W.L.

I Don't Dread This Journey, Odessa Steward, King Studio
    Chicago, Ill., 1946

I Have Made A Promise And I Can't Turn Around, pbc, 1946

I Know God Will Take Of Me, 1948, (Feat: Famous Golden
    Harps)

I Must Join That Heavenly Choir, 1947

I've Been Converted Thank You Jesus, 1948, (Feat: Famous
    Southern Echoes)

Just Didn't Mind Dying, pbc, 1946

Wasn't It A Pity How They Did My Lord, pbc, 1946

Felton, Pauline

My Soul Loves Jesus, pbc, Indianapolis, Ind., 1945

Ford, Herman James

    Abide Oh Lord With Me, An, 1954

    Everlasting Arms, An, 1951

    Everyday, RM, RM and pbc, 1956

    He Is Able, RM, 1946

    He Will Bring Joy To Your Soul

    He'll Hear And Answer Me, An, 1953

    He'll Meet Me One Day, An, 1953

    I Know I'll Be Ready To Go, pbc, 1955

    I Will Run, Run, Run To Jesus, KM, MM, 1947

    I'll Be At Rest, RM, 1946

    I'm Seeking For A City, RM, 1946

    In My Home Over There, RM, 1946

    Jesus Christ Is Born, An, 1950

    Jesus For Me, 1951

    Jesus Put A Song In My Soul, Martin Studio of Music, 1946

    Jesus Speaks To Me, An, 1953

    My Dream Of Heaven, An, 1953

    No Other Name, 1956, (Feat: Dorothy M. Raymond)

    None Of These Things Can Move Me, (Sung: Trinity Singers)

    Since Jesus Touched Me (Happy I Am), RM, 1946

    Tis The Hand Of The Lord, pbc, 1956

    Today And Always I Will Serve The Lord, MM, 1946

    Under His Care, An, 1953

    When All Is Said And Done, An, 1954

    When I Move Into The Kingdom, An, 1952

    Wonderful Savior, 1955, (Feat: Famous Lacy Moore Singers)

Frances, Cora

Lift Up Your Head, Jeanette Tall, 1948

Franklin, Rev. C.L.

I'm Not Ashamed To Own His Name, LB, 1942

Franklin, E.E.

Lord When I've Done The Best I Can, I Want My Crown, KM, LB, 1945

Frazier, Thurston G.

Come Holy Spirit, TFz and Voices of Hope, L.A. Calif., 1959

Fulton, Mary

The Lord Is My Shepherd, KM, MM, 1955

The Resurrection, 1955

Gage, A.F.

I'll Praise His Name (For Evermore), Gage Sr., Chicago, Ill., 1961

Gailes, Peggy L. Norfleet

I Know Jesus Will Save, pbc, 410 E. Pedagrew St. Durham, North Carolina, 1949

Gardner, Mary E.

I'll Take Jesus For Mine, TD, 1941

Gates, Molly N.

This Journey's Too Hard To Travel By Yourself, Bates, Chicago, Ill., 1948, (Ded: Rev. L. Body and his radio choir)

George, Casietta

He Never Left Me Alone, RM, 1959

George, Casietta (continued)

    I Believe In Thee, RM, MM, 1955, (Sung: Caravans)

    Ready To Serve The Lord, (Sung: Hyde Park Bible Church
        Radio Choir)

    Seek Ye The Lord, RM, 1959, (Ded: to her father, Rev.
        Peter Baker)

    These Things Must Be, KM, MM, 1960 (Rec: Caravans)

    To Whom Shall I Turn, MM, 1963, (Rec: Caravans)

    Waiting For Me, RM, 1955

    (Jesus Will Be) What You Want Him To Be, KM, MM, 1962

    Where Jesus Is, KM, MM, 1961

George, Herbert and Rev. Daisy Powell

    The Prize Is At The End, KM, Powell and George Music. Co.,
        1410 13th Ave., N. Minneapolis, Minn., 1962

Gerald, William

    Mother Pray For Your Son, pbc 1919 8th St. N.W., Washing-
        ton, D.C., 1951

    When I Get Through With My Toils And Care, Alice A. Fields,
        Washington, D.C., 1947

Gilliam, Margaret

    There Is Nothing That The Lord Cannot Do, KM, MM, 1955

Godwin, Daggat H.

    I See The Lord, H.D. Godwin Music Publ., Buffalo, N.Y.,
        1960

    It's Amazing, 1960

    Hear My Crown, 1959

    If You Believe, 1958

    Oh Lord I'm Saved, 1959

    Wonderful Is Jesus, 1957

Godwin, Deggat H. (continued)

    Welcome, 1959

Gooch, Mae

    Thank God, Amen, An, 1950, (Rec: Gospel Stars)

Goodman, Kenneth

    I've Just Come From The Fountain, International Copyright

Goodpasteur, Ralph H.

    After While It Will All Be Over, First Church of Deliver-
        ance 1960

    God Is, God Can, God Will, FCD, 1964

    God Has The Power, FCD, 1960

    He Heard My Cry, FCD, 1964

    He'll See You Through, FCD, 1953

    He's Real, FCD, 1955

    I Have Peace In My Heart Today, FCD, 1964

    I'm Saved And I Know That I Am, 1962

    I'm So Glad, So Glad, I'm So Glad, FCD, 1964

    Joy Bells Ringing In My Soul, FCD, 1961

    Lord I Am Grateful, 1959

    Oh Lord You Know, 1960

    Precious Is He, 1961

Goodson, Albert

    Jesus, Jesus, Jesus, KM, MM, 1958

    We've Come This Far By Faith, TFz, Goodson, 4211 So.
        Hooper Ave., L.A. Calif., 1959

Goodwin, Joe

    Bring Back Those Days

Goodwin, Joe (continued)

    God Is The Ruler Over Everything

    I'll Weather The Storm

    I've Been Saved

    I've Got The Holy Ghost

    Jesus Is Sweeter Than Honey

    Stand Up For Jesus

    Bring Down The Chariot

    That's How I Know Jesus

    What Did He Say?

Graham, Anne C.

    All To Jesus, An, 1950

    Are You Saved Today?, 1946

    Don't Worry About Him, 1949

    God Talks To Me

    Have You Talked To Me, 1944

    I Must Have Jesus All The Way, (Rec: Dixie Hummingbirds)

    I Must Work While It Is Day

    I Want The World To See Jesus In Me

    I Won't Turn Back

    Wasn't Jesus

    I've Got A Home In That Rock (Rec: Silverairs)

    Keep Me Lord And Fill My Heart With Fear, 1945

    Mother Mind

    Prayer Changes Things

    That Is Why My Soul Is Free

    There's A Better Day Coming

    Put Your Trust In Jesus

Graham, Anne C. (continued)

    The Old Account, RM

Green, Calvin Edward

    Jesus Is My Friend, LB, 1954

    Tell The Lord, LB, 1953

Green, Imogene

    How Could It Be, KM, MM, 1952, (Sung: James Cleveland
       Singers)

Green, Elder Washington

    After A While, pbc, 1952

Green, Willie A.

    He'll Answer You, pbc, 216 W. 100St., N.Y., 1962

Gregory, Billy

    Closer To Jesus, RM, Theola Brown, 178-38 131st Ave.,
       St. Albans, L.I., 1964

Griffin, Gloria

    The Gateway To Life, 1963, (Sung: Roberta Martin)

    God Specializes, RM, 1958, (Sung: Roberta Martin)

    I'm So Grateful, 1963

Gross, Thelma

    Then Lean On Me, Gross, Baltimore, Md., 1947

Fulton, Mary

    No Room At The Inn, KM, pbc, Chicago, Ill., 1955

Hall, Arby

    Wait Til Jesus Comes, KW, LB, 1961

Hall, Phyllis

    Count Me, RM, MM, 1949

    Just Wait A Little While, RM, 1950

    Let It Be Dear Lord Let It Be, RM, 1947

    This Dear Jesus For Me, VD, RM, 1945

Hall, Pernell Fleetwood

    I Am Traveling, Handy Brothers Music, 1587 Broadway,
       New York, N.Y., 1950

    Just Ask Jesus He Knows, HB

    Vengeance Is Mine, HB

    You Must Be Newborn Again, HB

    I Have Found My Lord A Savior, HB

    Life, Christian Travelers

    Triumphant Praise, I Talk With God, He Is Merciful He Is
       Great, HB

    I Will Lift Up Mine Eyes, HB

    Steal Away To Jesus, HB

    Go Down To Moses, HB

    I Am Seeking For A City, HB

    When I've Done My Best, HB

    The Battle Of Jerico, HB

    I've Been Buked, HB

    I'm So Glad That Trouble Don't Last Always, HB

    In That Great Getting Up Morning, HB

    Let Us All Bow Together, HB

    I'm On My Way, HB

    Ain't No Way's Weary, HB

Hall, Ruth

    The Gospel Of Salvation Is Real, Margarite Brown, MM, 1948

    I'm Working For A Crown Over There, MM, 1948

Hamilton, Eugene C.

    Christ Is The Answer, pbc, 1956

    I Am On My Journey Home, VD, pbc, Philadelphia, Pa, 1946

    I Will Meet You

    I'm Going Home Someday, (Ded: Sacred Heart Gospel Singers
       of Philadelphia, Pa.)

    In My Father's House, 1950

    No Night There, 1950

    Nothing But The Leaves, 1945

    Perfection, 1949

    We Will Shout The Harvest Home, 1947

    We Will Sing Hallelujah By And By, 1950

    Will You Be Waiting For Me, 1949, (Ded: to his son)

Harding, Mary L.

    I Know, pbc Bradakills, Pa., 1954

Harding, Sister Mae

    Ke'll Keep You, pbc, Ingster, Mich., 1949

    I Surrender, 1952

    God Leads Me I'll Go, 1950

    Jesus Has Brought Me All The Way, pbc, 1949

Harrell, Rev., A.L.

    I'm One Of Them, SEB Co., N.Y., 1944

Harris, Rev. E.

   Lord Entertain Me, 1961

Harris, Lola

   Holy Ghost Power, 1967, (Copies secured from owner,
      2910 W. Harrison St., Chicago, Ill.)

Harris, Mae Dell Owens

   I'll Live On, pbc 3111 Lipscomb St., Fort Worth, Tex., 1960

Harris, Mary Magdelene

   I Want Jesus To Smile On Me, 1949

   Jesus Is A Friend That Won't Forsake You, pbc, 1948

Harrison, Camele

   He's My Everything, RM, 1954, (Sung: Caravans)

Harrison, Hortense Lightfoot

   Glorify, MM, 1945

   A Right To Victory, MM, 1945

Hatcher, Clarence E.

   Come Let Us Walk Together In The Lord, pbc Brooklyn,
      New York, 1945, (Sung: Victory Gospel Singers)

   I Have Resolved To Keep The Faith, Hatcher Music House,
      1944

   I'll Be Caught Up To Meet Him In The Air

   Told The Bells In Zion, (Sung: Brown's Inspiration Singers)

Hatter, R.L. Sr.

   My Grace Is Sufficient For Thee, KM, Hatter and MM, 1951,
      (Sung: Senior Choir Mt. Moriah)

Hause, Edith Lucille

   He Is My Everything, pbc Denver, Colo., 1952

Hawkes, Zepheree

   Jesus Only, King Studio of Music, Chicago, Ill., 1944

Hawkins, Edwin R.

   Oh Happy Day, 1969

Hawthorne, Walter, Jr.

   Stop At The Saving Station, MM, 1952

Hayden, Debra Jereline

   Jesus My Guide, pbc, 1951, (Sung: Roberta Martin Singers)

   We Shall Go Home, RM, 1951

Hayes, Bertha O.

   Climbing Up The Mountain, pbc, Philadelphia, Pa., 1959

Heath, Mary Louise

   You Promise Me, pbc 650 West Alondra Blvd., Compton,
     Calif., 1957

Helms, Rebecca

   I'm Pressing On

   Land, Miller Music, 16 E. 18th Ave., Gary, Ind., 1950

Henderson, Lucille

   I'm Standing On The Rock, 1948, (Ded: Rev. L. Boddie,
     Greater Harvest Baptist Church, Chicago, Ill.)

   The Light Is My Guide, 1948, (Ded: Rev. C.H. Cobbs)

Henderson, N.G.

   I Give Up All My Sins And Serve The Lord, LB, 1937

Henderson, N.G. (continued)

    I'm Glad That I'm A Servant Of The Lord, LB, 1942

    Let Jesus Lead You All The Way, LB, 1941

    Now I'm So Glad I Got Good Religion, LB, 1939

    You've Got To Love Everybody, LB, 1938

Henderson, Rosa Lee

    Doctor Jesus, That's His Name, Altron Twig Music Studio,
        Memphis, Tenn., 1952

Hendon, Frank

    Every Prayer, pbc Indianapolis, Ind., 1945

    I Must Tell Jesus, 1945

    Jesus Is A Friend To You, Suzy B. Thompson, Indianapolis,
        Ind., 1945

Hendrix, Rev. S.P.

    I Know Jesus Will Be There, RM and Hendrix, 2234 E. 108
        St., Cleveland, Ohio, 1957

    I'm So Glad Jesus Is My Light, Mary Martin, 1957

Hendrix, James

    I Have A Father Who Can, Jermalean Music, Detroit, Mich.

    It Is Jesus, 1964

    In The End, 1950

    Just Now, 1963

    Let's Keep The Faith, Hendrix Studio, Nashville, Tenn.,
        1951

    Take My Hand, Jesus, Jesus, Holy One, Hendrix Studio, 1955

    Thank You Lord For Everything, Hendrix Studio, 1957
        (Feat: Hendrix Singers of Nashville and Sacred Tones)

    That's The Reason Why I Love Him Today, Hunt and Hendrix
        Studio

Hendrix, James (continued)

    When I See A Mountain, 1958

    Yesterday, 1957

Henry, Louis C.

    Mother Bowed, 1948, (Sung: Famous Pilgrim Travelers of
        L.A., Calif.)

Henry, Reuben

    I'm Still Living On Mother's Prayer, MM, 1950, (Rec:
        Soulstirrers)

    In That Awful Hour, 1950, (Rec: Soulstirrers)

Henry, Smithy

    I Don't Want Nobody To Keep Stumbling Over Me, MM, 1958,
        (Sung: Original Echoe Gospel Singers)

    I Have No Friend Like You, An, 1954, (Rec: Echoe Singers)

    I Want Jesus To Walk With Me, An, 1954

Herman, David

    Tis So Sweet, Savoy, 1959, (Sung: Corinthian Gospel
        Singers)

Herman, L.

    We Shall Be Changed, Savoy, 1959

Herndon, James

    God Is Here, LB, 1963, (Feat: Shirley Bell and the Sally
        Martin Singers, Delores Washington and the Caravans,
        Ded: Sally Martin)

    He Sits High And Looks Low, MM, 1962

    I Won't Be Back No More, 1962, (Sung: Caravans)

    I'm Satisfied I Found Peace At Last, MM, 1963, (Sung:
        Caravans)

    It's Good To Know Jesus, RM, 1962, (Sung: Caravans)

Herndon, James (continued)

    Keep Me Jesus, 1963, (Sung: Caravans)

    That's Why I Call Him Mine, MM, 1962, (Sung: Caravans)

    Till I Met The Lord, 1963, (Sung: Caravans)

Hicks, John B.

    Jesus Is All, Hicks, Crosby, Cleveland, Ohio, 1964, (Sung:
        Rasberry Singers)

Hill, Ada

    I Am Living On Borrowed Land, pbc, 418 NW 8th Ave., F.
        Lauderdale, Fla., 1964

    Tell It To Jesus, He Cares, pbc, 1964

Hill, Louise

    Come On To The Fold, LB, 1965

    Let The Master Use You

    My God Is A Magic Eye, 1965

Hilliard, Quency Mae

    Birth Of Christ, Hilliard Publ., 723 Taper Ave., Compton,
        Calif., 1963

    Yes Jesus Is Mine, 1963

Hines, Prof. J. Earle

    Blessed Be Thy Name, 1952, (Sung: Pilgrim Travelers)

    Come Ye Disconsolate, 1951

Hollowell, Bessemer Otha

    I Want To Go There, Don't You, Hunt and Hendrix, Nashville,
        Tenn., 1931

Holmes, Roman

    Resurrection, pbc Chicago, Ill., 1949

Holmes, Roman (continued)

What Manner Of Man Is This, Jackson Studio of Gospel
    Music, 4830 So. State St., Chicago, Ill., 1944

Holmes, Sara B.

Oh Lord Help Me I Pray, Holmes Music House, Houston,
    Texas, 1952

Hopkins, Georgia

We Hold The Lamb Of God, pbc, Hopkins Studio of Gospel
    Music, 2218 E. 46th St., Cleveland, Ohio, 1945,
    (Feat: Brown's Inspirational Singers)

Lord I'm A Soldier, KW, pbc, 1945

Hopkins, Bobby

I Know My Jesus Won't Deny Me, MM, LB, pbc, 1944

Hoyle, Winfred O.

I Know He Satisfied, LB, 1940

I'm So Glad Salvation's Free, W.O. Hoyle, LB, 1950

Jesus Walked The Water, LB, 1950

Jesus Walked This Lonesome Valley, W.O. Hoyle, 1952

Rock A My Soul, WOH, 1941

Saviour Thy Will Be Done, LB, 1948

Freedom Afterwhile, LB, 1948

He Can And Will Answer Prayer, LB, 1939

Hoyle, Prof. W. Olandis

Swiftly And Lowly I Come, MM, 1962

There's A Man Outside The Door, words, music LB and
    Winfred Hoyle, LB, 1955

When Trials Rise, LB, 1948

Hudson, L.J.

    I'll Trust Him On My Journey All The Way, W.D. David
       Gospel Studio of Music, 6125 Stanford St., Detroit,
       Mich., 1943

Hudson, R.E.

    At The Cross, MM, 1951

Hudson, Brother Wadell

    Dear Lord Hear My Plea, Gracey Mae Hilliard, 1962

Huff,   _____

    Yes I Know You Gonna Talk About Me, H and H Music Publ.,
       520 East 35th St., Chicago, Ill., 1948

Huffman, Rev. Eugene Henry

    Come And Dine, 1960

Hugg, George

    There's Not A Friend Like Jesus (No Not One, No Not One),
       VD, LB, 1948

    There's Not A Friend Like Jesus, RM, 1946

Huggins, William Frank

    It Will All Be Glory By And By, RM, 1947

    Won't It Be Beautiful, RM, 1947

Hunter, John G.

    I Come Dear Lord To Thee, LB, 1950

    I'm Climbing Higher Day By Day, KM, MM, 1949

Hurt, Amanda

    I'm Travelling, pbc Cleveland, Ohio, 1958

Husband, John J.

   Hallelujah (Revive Us Again), MM, 1958 (Sung: Sally Martin)

Hutchinson, Theresa

   There's Peace In The Valley For Me, Martin Studio Gospel
       Music, 1945

Hyemingway, Rhoda

   What Is Life Without Christ, Rev. Walter Louis Gospel
       Music Studio, 2314 S. Central Ave., Los Angeles,
       Calif., 1955

Isel, Will

   My Prayer To Thee, words Bob Level, LB, 1950

Jackson, Emma L.

   I Can See Everybody's Mother But I Can't See Mine, pbc
       Jackson Music Studio, 4830 S. State St., Chicago,
       Ill., 1945

   Jesus Never Fails, pbc, 1944, (Sung: Jackson Singers)

Jackson, A.

   As Long As Jesus Lives, Jackson Music Co., 703 S. 14th
       St., Birmingham, Ala.

Jackson, James Albert

   Guide Me Lord I Pray, 1947, (Sung: Golden Tone Singers)

   I'm Walking With My Lord, 1947

Jackson, Katherine Cecelia

   I've Got A Savior, Coleman Studio of Gospel Music, 8517
       Cedar Ave., Cleveland, Ohio, (Feat: Wilson Jubilee
       Singers)

Jackson, Myrtle

   But Just I Pray Oh Lord Remember Me, Myrtle Jackson, RM,
       1944

Jackson, Myrtle

    Can You Carry Your Burdens To Jesus

    Come To Jesus (Right Now)

    He Lifted Me Somewhere

    Look Up To Jesus

    Jesus Is A Rock

    But This I Pray Oh Lord

    Remember Me

    I'm Glad To Know I Am In His Will, Myrtle Jackson Studio
        of Gospel Music, South Michigan Blvd., Chicago, Ill.,
        1946

    Come To Jesus Face To Face, 1948

    He Didn't Mind Dying, 1950

    He Lifted Me, 1941, (Sung: Roberta Martin)

    He Sure Is Good To Me, 1941

    I Promised I'd Serve Him (Going To Keep My Word), 1941

    I Want To Be Ready, 1941

    I'll Work For The Lord, 1941, (Ded: First Church of
        Deliverance)

    I'm Living By Faith And Grace

    It's So Important (That I Make It In), 1947

    Jesus Is A Rock, VD, 1945

    Let The Hand of Jesus Lead You Through, Jackson, LB,
        1940

    Oh Yes I Want To Make A Soldier

    Oh Yes I'm Free, 1940

    Praise The Lord He's Alright Now, 1940

    Somewhere, 1945

    There's Nothing Like The Holy Spirit, 1946

    When My Tears Are Falling Down, 1950

Jackson, Myrtle (continued)

    Where Can I Go But To The Lord, 1951

    Where Jesus Leads Me (I Will Follow), 1947

James, Dorothy J.

    Worthy Is The Land, pbc, 8005 S. Yale Ave., Chicago, Ill., 1964

James, Ella Mae

    Just Jesus And I, 1957

James, Hamilton

    I Love My Lord, pbc and MM, 1944

James, Jessie

    I Need The Lord To Go All The Way, Jackson Music, Birmingham, Ala., 1946

Jenkins, Sister Elizabeth M.

    I Need The Dear Jesus, pbc 1720 N. Mount St., Baltimore, Md., 1946

    If Jesus Comes What Then, 1946

    It Is Sweet To Walk With Jesus, 1946

    Praise Jesus Name, 1946

    So It Pays To Be Ready When Jesus Comes

    That Holy City Will Be My Home

Jeter, Claude A.

    He Won't Deny Me, MM, 1953 (Sung: Swan Silvertones)

    I'm Coming Home, 1953

    It Won't Be Long, Sylvia Boddie Studio, 5121 S. State St., Chicago, Ill., 1950 (Ded: Rev. Boddie and Greater Harvest Choir)

Johnson, Clara Lee

    Jesus Said Not, pbc 1715 E. 54th St., Los Angeles, Calif.,
       1948

Johnson, Miss Clyde

    I Want To Come A Little Closer Lord To Thee, MM, 1949

    Jesus My Soul Shall Walk With Thee, MM, 1948

Johnson, Isam

    By And By I Will See Jesus, pbc, St. Louis, Missouri, 1945

    Faith And Grace Is All I Need, pbc, 1943

    I Just Stand And Ring My Hands And Cry, 1944

    I Know The Lord Can Heal My Body and Soul, 1945

    I Want You To Know About Jesus, Yes I Do, 1945

    I'm Going To Live Right On, 1945

    Let Us Run To Jesus Everyone, 1945

    Someday I'll See My Saviour's Face So Bright, 1945

Jones, Arthur Eugene

    I'll Reach My Home Someday, Jones Studio Music, 2646
       Loretta Ave., Baltimore, Md., 1945

    Lead Me To The Rock, LB, 1943

    Tabernacle Of The Lord, Nat'l. Gospel Workers Aid Society,
       Baltimore, Md., 1946

Jones, Betty

    Won't It Be Grand, KM, 1944

Jones, Beulah Vesta

    He Lifted Me, pbc, 123 W. 41st Pl., L.A., Calif., 1962

Jones, Elizabeth Hall

    Put Your Trust In Jesus, 1950

Jones, Estell Manning

    Wonderful Jesus And Shelter Of Love, pbc East Chicago,
       Indiana, 1951

Jones, Harman William

    When I Quit The Devil I'm Glad I'm Saved, 1952, (The
       Lacy Gospel Singers and Heavenly Harmony)

Jones, Isiah

    He Will Make Everything Better For You, MM, 1964

    I Just Can't Get Along Without You, KM, MM, 1961, (Sung:
       Cassietta George and the All Stars)

    I Thank God, MM, 1959

    I'm An Heir, Robert Anderson, GS, 1957, (Feat: Robert
       Anderson Singers of Chicago, Ill.)

    I've Got Jesus, 1957

    Let Him In, 1962

    My Soul Feels All Right, 1956

    Never Will He Turn His Back On Me, MM, 1964, (Sung: James
       Cleveland, The Caravans and other leading singers)

    No Matter What I Do (He's There To Guide Me), MM, 1958

    Thank Him For Everything, MM, 1960

    To Him I Belong, RM, 1959

    As For Me And My Household We'll Serve The Lord, MM, 1956

    You Ought To Serve Him (While It's Time), MM, 1962

Jones, James H.

    God Will Answer Prayer, MM, 1961

Jones, James F.

    He Is Our Saviour, J.P. Powell, Chicago, Ill., 1948

Jones, Patricia

   In Your Name Lord I Come, pbc 202 1/2 Hinckle, Columbus,
      Ohio, 1963

Jones, Paul Curtis

   Jesus Is My Friend, 1951

   The Man I Long To See, pbc 20804 Garden Land, Ferndale,
      Mich., 1950

Jones, Sallie

   Standing In The Safety Zone, MM, 1942

Jones, Willard

   Do You Know Jesus (He's A Friend Of Mine), LB, 1954

   Have Faith In God, LB, 1954

   I Want To Thank Him, LB, 1954

   My Troubles Will Be Over, LB, 1952

   I Talk With The Lord, LB, 1954

   What Jesus Said, LB, 1954

Jones, Willie D.

   Don't Let Satan Keep You Away, Livingston Studio, Balti-
      more, Md., 1946

Joyner, Ella Mae

   Let Us Work While It Is Day, pbc, Washington, D.C., 1949

Kaiser, Pearl Joseph

   Everlasting Praise Of The Saved, JT, MM, 1945

Kendrix, A.L.

   This Is What I Do, LB, 1938

   When The Pearly Gates UnFold, LB, 1938

Kennedy, David

    Beautiful City, pbc 2000 Fawcett Ave., McKeesport, Pa.,
       1950

    Going Home Some Day, 1950

King, Janie

    I Found A Favor In Christ, VD, 1951

    Ever And Ever Close To Thee, VD, 1951

King, Marie

    Saviour Of The World, pbc 66 Spruce St., Stamford, Conn.,
       1959

King, R.   (All entries published by MM but through an
         arrangement with Pathway House of Music)

    Just In Time, 1963, (Sung: Alice Bradford)

    Let The Lord Be Seen In You, Pathway House of Music, 1963

    One Step, words by Prof. Alex Bradford, Pwy., 1963

    Walk Through The Streets, Pwy., 1963

    What About You, Pwy., 1963

Knapp, Mrs. Joseph F.

    Blessed Assurance Jesus Is Mine, LB, 1951

Knox, Odell

    You Got To Know God To Love Him, pbc Memphis, Tenn., 1962

Lafayette, Ollie

    Don't Forget To Pray, Atkins and Lafayette, Chicago, Ill.,
       1961

    Everything I Do (In Jesus Name), pbc Lafayette Music House,
       438 E. 93rd St., Chicago, Ill., 1965, (Rec: Helen
       Robinson Youth Choir)

    Feel Me Lord I Want To Be Thine, 1952

Lafayette, Ollie (continued)

    God Is Everywhere, 1961

    God Will Bless You, 1961

    God Is Calling You, 1961

    The Hand Of God, 1961, (Rec: Mahalia Jackson)

    I Want To Be Worthy, 1961

    I'll Go, 1958

    I've Got Jesus (In My Soul), 1965

    I've Got To Keep Running, 1961

    Joy To Praise His Name, 1961

    Just Keep Jesus In Your Life, 1959

    Lord, You Brought Me Out, 1964

    Not A One, 1959

    Only God, 1965

    Precious Jesus (Hungry Souls Prayer), 1965

    Seek Ye The Lord, 1964

    Teach Me The Way, 1959

    Where Jesus Is It Is Heaven, 1961

    Yes Lord You Know My Heart, 1969

Lafon, Rev. H.

    A Glorious Time, MM, 1960

    Step By Step

    I'm Going To Run This Christian Race, pbc 2920 S. State
       St., Chicago, Ill., 1964

Lattirmer, Alice R.

    He Walks With Me, 1962

    I Wondered Wondered, Wondered, 1960

    Wonderful Joy, pbc, 1960

Lattirmer, Leonettza

    I Want To Go To Heaven When I Die, Miller's Studio of
        Music, Gary, Ind., 1956

Lavalley, Artie Mrs.

    I Can Do All Things Through Christ, MM, 1966

Lawson, Mariam

    He's Listening To My Prayer, pbc California, 1955

    That's Why I Love Him So, RM, 1949

Leet, L.W.E. James

    I've Tried Jesus, LB, 1955

    My Gold, RM, 1955

Lewis, Harold

    God Is Looking Down On You, MM, 1961, (Sung: Harold Lewis
        Coraleers, Aquarium Music, Hattisburg, Miss.)

    I Know I've Got Religion, RM, 1965

Lewis, Samuel Alan

    An Angel In Heaven, LB, approx. 1953

    A Beacon Light, LB, MM, 1950

    Christ Is My All And All, LB, MM, 1955

    Cross Out On The Lonely Hill, 1954

    Don't Turn Around, MM, 1950

    A Friend Like Jesus, 1957

    Go Ahead, Go Ahead, LB, 1950

    God's Christmas Gift To The World, MM, 1956

    He Shows Me The Way, LB, 1950

    Hear My Prayer, Amen, LB, 1948

    Heaven's Highway, LB, 1954

Lewis, Samuel Alan (continued)

He's All Right With Me, LB, 1949

Hold The Light, 1956, (Sung: Little Lucy and the Smith
    Singers)

I Found Out, LB, 1954

I Know Jesus, What About You, 1951

I Know My Name's On High, VD, TF, 1947

I Want Jesus To Be My Guiding Light, LB, 1954

If You Make A Start In Jesus' Name (Go On Through), LB,
    1954

I'll Serve Jesus, TF, 1948

I'm Going To Live By God's Word, LB, 1950

I'm Going To Tell The World Why Jesus Died, VD, TF, 1947

I'm Heaven Bound, MM, 1950

In The Land Of Endless Day, LB, 1950

It's A Might Hard Road, MM, 1954

I've Got A River To Cross, MM, 1955

Jesus, Brighten Up My Life, MM, 1955

Jesus, I Love To Call Your Name, 1951

Jesus Is The Mercy Seat, LB, 1951

Jesus Is The Search Light, 1947

Jesus Paid The Debt, 1955

Jesus The Waymaker, 1949

Jesus Was The One, 1951

Jesus Went This Way Before, MM, 1953, (Sung: Violettia
    Walker Soloist St. Paul Gospel Choral Unit)

Just Live Right For Yourself, LB, 1950

The Lord Has Set Me Free, LB, 1947

Lord I Need You Every Day Of My Life, MM, 1951

Lord Will I Find Peace Someday?, MM, 1953

Lewis, Samuel Alan (continued)

    The Man Behind The Clouds, 1956

    My Mind Is Saved On Jesus, MM, 1957

    My Record Is On High, MM, 1947

    No, No, Noah Said, LB, 1950

    Oh Lord, Oh Lord, VD, TF, 1947

    A Servant In God's Kingdom Is All I Want To Be, LB, 1950

    There Is A Fountain Filled With Blood, words Wm. Cowper,
        S. Lewis, LB, 1953

    We Are Born To Die, LB, VD, 1951

    When Jesus Comes To Claim His Own, Viola Dicken, LB, 1950

Lewis, Elder Walter

    I'm Glad That Jesus Lives, pbc L.A. Calif., 1951

    Until Jesus My Saviour Shall Come, pbc, 1951

Lewis, Magnolia Butts

    Breath On Me, TF, RM, LB, 1941

Lindsy, Eleanor

    I'm Safe In The Ark From The Storm, Battle and Odum
        Sacred Music Composers, 1541 75th St., Wash. D.C.,
        1946

    Lord I'll Follow In Your Footsteps All The Way

Lindsy, Winnetta

    I'll Be So Glad, TF, 1951

    Oh Jerusalem And Worth Is The Land

Lucas, Harvey W.

    Your Final Decision, pbc Phila. Pa., 1947

Lumkins, Leon

    Behind Every Dark Cloud, 1960, (Rec: Gospel Clefts
        Playmar Music Co.)

    Open Our Eyes, 1959

    Out Of The Fiery Furnace, 1960

    Rise Up And Walk, 1959

    Wings Of A Dove, Savoy, 1958

Lytle, Evangelist J.F.

    He Came To Set Us Free, Quincy Mae Hilliard, 1963

    Now With God, 1963

McCain, Rev. Agnes

    Just Wait A Little While, 1949

    Feed Me Jesus And Peace Be Unto You

McClain, Truzella

    So Glad He Is My Guide, 1954

McClellan, Andrea

    Just As Long As I Live I Will Serve Him, LB, 1963, (Feat:
        S. Martin)

McCoy, Nellie

    All Over Me Like A Burning Fire, pbc Decator, Mich., 1959

    A Wonderful Saviour For Me

McCree, Leonard

    Make Me Lord What You Want Me To Be, pbc Camden, Ard.,
        1964

McDonald, Louise

    I Love The Lord, RM, 1959

McDonald, Louise (continued)

    I Need You Lord (Right Now)

    I'm Going To Trust Him Everyday, (Sung: Caravans)

    It's My Plan, (Sung: Caravans)

    Rest For The Weary, (Sung: Caravans, Gospel Harmony, Soul-
        Stirrers and other leading groups)

    There's Rest For The Weary, MM, 1955

McDonald, Marcus

    I'm Homeward Bound, pbc Milwaukee, Wis., 1957

McGee, Myrtle

    Blessed Is The Name, Myrtle's Music House, Gary, Ind., 1952

    Just Keep Me Humble

McGee, Morris

    Satisfied, RM, 1949, (Sung: Original Hutchins Trumpeteers)

McKinney, R. Lee

    Free At Last, Lee's Mart Music, Buffalo, N.Y., 1960

    Wonderful Is His Name

Livingston, Isador Jordon

    Beautiful City, pbc Baltimore, Md., 1945

    My Lord Is Calling

Love, Dorothy (Published by MM, or Ve; entries copyrighted
               1954-1960, most entries arranged by Kenneth
               Morris)

    Don't You, (Sung: Orig. Gospel Harmonettes)

    Elijah

    The Finishing Line

    God's Goodness (You Don't Know How Good God Is To Me)

Love, Dorothy (continued)

    He's Calling

    He's Calling Me

    He's Right On Time

    I Shall Know Him

    I Wouldn't Mind Dying

    I'll Be With Thee

    Jesus Laid His Hand On Me

    Let Me Ride

    Lord Don't Forget About Me

    Ninety Nine And One Half

    No Hiding Place

    One Morning Soon

    So Many Years

    That's Enough

    The Walls Of Jerico Must Come Down

    When I Reach My Heavenly Home On High

    Where Shall I Be

    Who Art Thou

    We Must Be Born Again

Love, Elmo C.

    Jesus Lifted Me, LB, 1954

Love, Donald M.

    I'm Packing Up, pbc Alaquippa, Pa., 1955

    I'm Bound For Canaan To The Land Of Light

Lowe, Ora

    The Morning Soon Will Be Dawn, VD, LB, 1952

Lowe, Ora (continued)

    The Saviour Is Calling Me

Lowry, Robert

    I Need Thee Every Hour, Dorothy Atkins

Maddox, Fannie

    Because You've Been So Good To Me, 1952

    He Satisfied My Soul, AC, 1963, (Sung: Northeastern State
        Choir - Church of God In Christ, Detroit, Mich.)

    Jesus What A Wonderful Friend He Is

Mann, Columbus

    Shall Be Mine, Jean and L Music and Record Mart, Detroit,
        Mich., 1960, (Feat: State Choir, South Western COGIC)

Markum, Henry Payne

    I Know He Cares For Me, 1952, (Sung: Willa Mae Ford Smith,
        and Cora Martin)

Martin, Cora

    All That I Need Is In Jesus, pbc 4315 So. Central Ave.,
        L.A., Calif., 1959

    Deliver Me Oh Lord

    Do You Know The Lord Jesus For Yourself

    He Is A Friend Of Mine

    Heaven Sweet Heaven

    Just Call His Name

    Keep Your Heart In Tune

    Oh Lord Show Me The Way, (Rec: Voices of Hope, Thurston
        Frazier, Director)

    A Prayer Wheel Turning In My Heart

    Trust In Jesus, (Feat: Cleophus Robinson)

Martin, Cora (continued)

    What A Wonderful Saviour I Found

    The Lord Is On The Stormy Sea

Martin, Roberta Evelyne

    The Angels Are Hovering Around, 1950

    Any Time, 1960

    The Best Things In Life Are Free, 1963

    Brighten The Way, 1963

    Child Of God, 1966

    Did You Thank Him, 1962

    Each Day I Grow A Little Nearer, 1948

    Everybody Won't Get There, 1945

    God Can Do Everything, 1965

    God's Amazing Grace, 1938

    God's Love (It Reaches Me), 1961

    He Never Said A Word, 1954

    He's Always Giving, 1965

    He's Always There, 1954

    He's Merciful, 1963

    How Long Has It Been Since You Prayed, 1958

    I Hear God, 1962

    I Want The World To See Jesus In My Life, 1950

    If You Pray, 1960

    I'll Take Jesus On My Journey, 1950

    I'm Going To Follow In His Footsteps, 1949

    I'm Going To Run To Jesus (He'll Be My Hiding Place)

    I'm Just Waiting On The Lord, 1953

    In God Confide, 1963

Martin, Roberta Evelyne (continued)

    God Is Still On The Throne, 1959

    God Will Deliver You, 1964

    He Never Said, 1954

    In My Heart, 1954

    Is There Anyone Here Who Loves Jesus, 1953

    I've Got To Cross Over To See My Lord, 1949

    Keep Me In Touch With Thee, 1964

    Looking Back, 1959

    Lord I Won't Turn Back, 1959

    Will You Shall I, 1951

    Who Is He, 1964

    Where You Going To Run To, 1956

    When He Died, 1956

    What Kind Of Man Is This, 1954

    Walk On (One Step At A Time), 1961

    Try Jesus, 1960

    To Jesus I'll Always Go, words and music James Cleveland,
       RM, 1961

    They'll Be Joy, 1965

    That's Why I Love Him Today, 1963

    Swing Down Chariot, 1956

    Standing In The Need Of Prayer, 1956

    Soon I Will Be Done With The Troubles Of The World

    Since He Lightened My Heavy Load, 1954

    Shine Heavenly Light, 1954

    Search My Heart, LB, 1935

    Say - Are You Ready?, 1951

    Saviour Lead Me On, 1940

Martin, Roberta Evelyne (continued)

    Only God, 1960

    Only By Grace, 1962

    Oh Say So (Tell His Love Today), 1945

    Oh I Want Jesus To Walk With Me, 1938

    No Other Help I Know, 1961

    My Soul, 1955

    My Friend, 1949

    My Eternal Home, 1947

    More Than All, 1954

Martin, Rosa Lee

    Have You Tried Him, RM, James Cleveland, 1947

    I'll Be So Happy When His Dear Faith I Shall See

Martin, Sallie

    Great Day (When Jesus Christ Was Born), KW, 1961

    (Following entries, words and music by Thomas Dorsey and Sallie Martin:)

    He Has Gone To Prepare A Place For Me, 1934

    He's Coming Again, 1954

    I Tried Jesus And I Know, KM, SM, MM, 1946

    I Still On The Glory Roll, LB, 1958

    Just A Few Days To Label, MM, 1944

    Nearer Oh Lord To Thee, 1956

    Speak Lord Jesus, 1955 (Sung: Brother Joe May)

    The Sweetest Name I Know, 1961

    Wonderful Is His Name, 1957

    You're Not Walking Alone, 1954, (Sung: Brother Joe May)

Martin, W.S.

    God Will Take Care Of You, 1951, (Sung: Roberta Martin
        Singers)

Matthews, Lucy Elaine (or Little Lucy), (All published by RM)

    Beautiful Robes, 1950

    Come On To Me, 1955

    He Has Done Great Things

    He'll Never Let Go My Hand

    He's My Light

    Tha Man of Calvery

    He's So Divine

    He's The One, 1950

    I Just Had To Call His Name, 1955

    I'm A Witness For My Lord, 1965 (Sung: Roberta Martin
        Singers)

    I've Got A Home For You, 1963

    Oh What A Time, 1950

    There Is A God (Who Understands), 1955

    There's None Like Him, 1952

    This I Do Believe, 1966

    Walk In The Beautiful Light Of God, 1950

    What A Blessing In Jesus I Found, 1949

    Whisper A Prayer, 1965

Means, _____

    If I Walk With Him, TD, 1963

    I'm Saved Through Faith By Grace, KM, 1964

Mitchell, Austin

    Hallowed Be Thy Name, music by Mitchell Wdby, RM, 1946

Mitchell, Nancy Childress

    Jesus Saviour I Adore Thee, pbc Palesky, Va., 1949

Mitchell, Willie

    Lord Let Me Walk In The Path Of Righteousness, pbc
       Robbins, Ill., 1959

Monroe, Cordilia

    Climbing The Golden Stairs, Monroe Music House, Va., 1945

    Heaven Is A Beautiful Place, 1945

    Humble Thyself To Walk With God, 1946

    I Want The World To See Jesus In My Life, VD, 1946

    I'll Be All Right, 1944

    Is It Well With Your Soul, 1944

    It's All Right Now, 1945

    I've Got Jesus In My Soul, 1950

    All The Way

    My Life Is In His Hand, 1950

    When I Come To The Sunset Gate, 1950

    You Know Your Mother Always Cared For You, 1945

Moore, Daniel A. Rev.

    Step By Step, Mae A. Moore, 1957

Moore, Ella Mae Mitchell

    The Golden Gate, pbc L.A. Calif., 1943

Moore, Elma Opal

    Speak To Me Jesus, First Church of Deliverance, 1956

Moore, Mary E. Lacy

    I Find Joy In Telling The World What Jesus Has Done For
        Me, Mary Harris, Norfolk, W.V., 1949

Moore, Roosevelt

    A Child Is Born, An, 1953

Morganfield, Willie

    Can I Ride

Morris, Kenneth

    I'll Overcome Someday, 1945

Morris, Mrs. C.H.

    Let Jesus Come Into Your Heart, LB, 1963, (Rec: S. Martin
        Singers)

    Sweeter As The Years Go By

    What If It Were Today

    Almost Home, 1957, (Rec: Famous Davis Sisters)

    Amazing Grace, (Sung: Soulstirrers)

    Left And Brought Up By The Lord

    Bless His Name

    Certainly Lord

Morris, Kenneth

    You Must Have That True Religion

    Christ Is All, 1947

    Come Home And I Come To Thee, 1947

    Come On Today, 1958

    Come Ye Disconsolate, 1948

    Crucified, 1952

    Day By Day, 1951

Morris, Kenneth (continued)

Dig A Little Deeper In God's Love, 1948

Does Jesus Care, 1945

Ease My Troubling Mind, 1953

Every Time I Feel The Spirit, 1953

I Have Not Seen (Just What The Lord Has In Store For You), 1949

Glory, Glory Hallelujah, 1949, (Sung: Soulstirrers)

God Will Take Care Of You, 1951, (Ded: Gay Sisters)

God's Got His Eyes On You, 1953

Soon I Will Be Done With Troubles And Going Home To Live With God, (Sung and Rec: Jessy Dixon, James Cleveland and the Gospel Chimes)

Hallelujah Tis Done, 1961, (Sung: Caravans)

Have You Any Rivers, 1958

He Answered Me, 1946

He Never Has Left Me Alone, (Sung: Spirits Quartet)

He Will Give Me Rest, (Feat: S. Martin and M&M Singers)

He's Holding My Hand

Hold To God's Unchanging Hand, (Sung: J. Cleveland Singers, new arrangement)

He's My Rock, My Sword, My Shield

I'm Going To Work Until My Day Is Done

It Is Well With Your Soul, (Sung: Caravans)

I'm Walking With My Jesus, 1943

I Am Weak But I'm Willing, 1958

I Can Put My Trust In Jesus, 1941

I Can't Turn Around, 1953 (new arrangement)

I Had A Talk With Jesus, 1954

I Have Something Within Me (It Must Be Jesus' Love Divine), 1959

Morris, Kenneth (continued)

I Know God, words Brunson, San Pedro, Calif., 1963

I Know It Was The Blood, (Sung: Voice of Tabernacle, Dir.
    by James Cleveland

I Know That I'll Overcome, 1947

I Live For Jesus, 1960

I Must Tell Jesus, Shaw Bros., Evanston, Ill., 1944, (Sung:
    Shaw Brothers)

I See Him, 1957

I Thank The Lord, 1944, (Sung: Sally Martin)

I Just Want To Be Dear Lord, 1944

I Want To Go Where Jesus Is, 1943

I Will Give You Rest, 1950

I'll Overcome Some Day, 1945

I Woke Up This Morning (With My Mind Stayed On Jesus),
    1955

I Won't Have To Cross The River Of Jordan All Alone, 1946

If You Trust Him, 1963

I'll Let Nothing Separate Me From His Love, 1940

I'm Going To Bury Myself In Jesus' Arms, 1945

I'm Going To Follow Jesus, 1949

I'm Going To Move In The Room With The Lord, 1951

I'm Going To Move On Up A Little Higher, (Sung: Soul-
    stirrers)

I'm Going To Tell The World Why Jesus Died On Calvary,
    1952

I'm Ready To Do Thy Will, 1946

I'm Singing Glory To His Name, 1951

I'm Waiting On The Lord, 1941, (Feat: S. Martin)

Is It Well With Your Soul, 1944, (Sung: Angelic Choir,
    Antioch Baptist Church, Chicago, Ill.)

Morris, Kenneth (continued)

It's A Highway, A Slow Way, A Hard Trip Up To Heaven,
     1954, (Dorothy Dixon and the Gospel Chimes)

It's So Wonderful To Have A Friend Like Jesus, 1954

It's Worth It, 1941

I've Been On This Road And I'm Not Tired Yet, 1950

I've Got An Interest Over There, 1943

Jesus Has Traveled On This Road Before, 1948

Jesus Is Mine, 1947

Jesus Is The Answer To Every Problem, 1954

Jesus Is The Only One, 1949

Jesus Is The Ruler Of My Life, 1944

Jesus Met The Women At The Well, words J.W. Alexander,
     1949, (Sung: Pilgrim Travelers)

Jesus Prayed For You And I, 1944

Jesus Steps Right In Just When I Need Him Most, (Feat:
     Golden Harps Quartet)

Jesus Will Be With Me In My Dying Hour, 1940

Just Like Jesus, 1946

King Jesus Will Roll All Burdens Away, 1947

Let Jesus Come Into Your Soul, 1953

The Light Of The World Is Jesus, 1952

Look For Me In Heaven I'll Be There, 1944

Lord I'm Your Child

My Life Is In His Hand, (Rec: Skylard Soulsters,
     Harmonizing Chorus, Sensational Nightingales)

Lord When I've Done The Best I Can I Want My Crown, LB,
     1945

The Lord Be With You All The Way, 1946

Makes No Difference What You Think Of Me, 1945

Morris, Kenneth (continued)

Mary Don't You Weep, (Sung and Feat: Inez Andrews and the Caravans)

The Moment I Met Jesus, 1949

Most Of All I'm Going Home To See My Lord, 1948

My God Is Real (Yes God Is Real), 1944

My Hope Is Built, music Bradbury and Edward Mote, KM, (Sung: Caravans)

My Jesus Rose, 1951, (Sung: S. Martin Singers)

My Jesus Won't Leave Me Alone, 1950

(I'm Worried) My Time Ain't Long, 1959, (Sung: Mighty Gospel Giants, Swan Silvertones, Nightingales and the Staple Singers)

Oh Lord I Come To Thee, 1954

One Day, 1946

Open Up The Pearly Gates, 1949

Prayer And A Little Faith, 1953

Resting Under The Shadow of God's Wing, 1948

Sign Of The Judgement, 1953

Some Glad Happy Day, 1947

Some Day, In Due Time, 1952

Sometime, 1953, (Feat: Sally Martin)

Steal Away To Jesus, 1953, (Sung: Five Soulstirrers)

(Everyday With Jesus) Sweeter Than The Day Before, (Sung: Famous Gospel Allstars)

Take All To Jesus, 1953

Thank You Jesus, 1948, (Sung: Soulstirrers)

That Old Time Religion, KM

There's No Sorrow That Heaven Cannot Heal, 1950

The Day Christ Was Born, LB, 1938

Morris, Kenneth (continued)

   Well, Well, Well, Don't Worry About Me, 1953, (Sung:
       Soulstirrers)

   We're Marching To Zion, Choral Arr. KW, 1953, (Sung:
       Bradford)

   What He's Done For Me, 1958, (Rec: Famous Davis Sisters)

   When I Join That Jubilee, 1949, (Sung: Prof. James Earl
       Hines)

   When I Reach That City Over There, 1947

   When The Love Came Trickling Down, 1949

   Will You Be There (I Will Be There), 1948

   Yes, I Want To Rest, Orig. words James Sands, 1947

   You Better Run, 1956, (Sung: Orig. Gospel Harmonettes,
       new version)

   You Must Be Born Again, 1953

Morrison, Lonnie

   I'm Pressing Forward, Pastor of Antioch Bapt. Church,
       Brooklyn, N.Y., 1952

Moss, Bill

   Just The Two Of Us, AC, 1965, (Sung: Bill Moss and the
       Celestials)

   My New Determination, 1965

Motley, Mary Lou

   Hold Me Jesus In Thine Arms, Motley's Gospel Music Shop,
       Detroit, Mich., 1944

   I'm Determined To Go In The Name Of The Lord

   Lead Me On Jesus Let Me Stand, 1945

Moultire, Willa Ward

   Who Shall Be Able To Stand, Moultrie, Wards House of Music,
       Phila., Pa., 1953, (Sung: Famous Ward Sisters)

Moyer, Evelyne

    All To Thee, LB, 1952

    Here I Am, RM, 1952

    I Don't Mind, RM, 1951

    I Found Rest, RM, 1951

    Keep On Knocking, LB, 1952

    No One Loves Me Like Jesus, RM, 1952

Nedd, _____

    Did You Really See Jesus, Nedd, Cleveland, Ohio, 1945
       (Feat: Heavenly Gospel Singers of Alabama)

    I Know The Lord Always Will Provide A Way For You, 1945

    I'm Going To Fight With The Staff In My Hands, 1945

    Jesus Is A Friend To Everyone

    Did You Really See Jesus, Nedd, Cleveland, Ohio, 1945
       (Feat: Heavenly Gospel Singers)

    I Know The Lord Will Always Provide A Way For You, 1945

    My Jesus Said, 1944 (special arrangement)

    Our Father, words, music Nedd, 1947

    Yes I Feel Thy Power Divine Everyday, 1944

Neugin, J.W. Sr. and Jr.

    I've A Mansion In Heaven, It's Promised To Me, Staff Publ.
       Co., Chicago, Ill., 1960

Nickleberry, Octavia

    Stormy Night, pbc Detroit, Mich., 1945

Norwood, Dorothy

    All Things Are Possible, 1960

    Can You Walk (How Blessed You Are), 1960, (Sung: Caravans)

    Come On Jesus, 1957

Norwood, Dorothy (continued)

Have Mercy On Me, 1958, (Sung: Gospel Chimes)

Have You Stopped To Count Your Blessings, 1961

He Laid His Hands On Me, 1959

I Cried Lord Please Move These Things That's Worrying Me,
     1958, (Feat: Staple Singers)

I'm Building My Mansion In Heaven (The Deeds Will Be Mine),
     1958

I'm Saved

Jesus Is My Rock, 1964

Just Like Fire Shut Up My Bones, 1961

Lord Remember Me, 1957, (Sung: Caravans)

Meeting Tonight, 1957, (Sung: Caravans)

My Soul Looks Back And Wondered, 1959

(You Ought To) Show Some Sign, 1957, (Sung: Caravans)

Step In Jesus, 1958

Well, Well, Well, 1958, (Sung: Swan Silvertones and the
     Caravans)

You've Got To Be Real, 1957, (Sung: Caravans)

You've Got To Move, 1957

Olds, Geneiva

I Have A Home, Dorsey and Olds, Chicago, Ill., 1956

Paste, Charles H. (Entries listed below published by Old Ship
                    of Zion Publishing House, Pittsburgh,
                    Pennsylvania)

Just As I Journey On, 1944

Because of You, 1949

Bread Of Heaven Feed Me Till I Want No More, 1945

Everybody Will Be Happy When The Saints Go Marching In,
     1945

Paste, Charles H. (continued)

Go, Go Tell It Everywhere, 1953

Come To Return No More, 1948

He Is Real, 1944

He Is Sweeter As The Years Roll By

He Keeps The Fire Burning Down In My Soul

He Will Say Well Done Someday, 1947, (Sung: Evangelist
   Lewis Banks)

He's Often A Maker To Me, 1949

He's Everything To Me He's All Right, 1947

I Must Tell Jesus All, 1947

I Promise The Lord, 1945

I Shouted, Joy, Joy, Joy, 1956

I'm Born Again

I'm Going To Hold To The Cross Till I Die

I'm Going To Walk And Talk With My Jesus Someday, 1945

I Am On My Way To Heaven Shouting On, 1945

In That Morning, 1945

In That New Jerusalem, 1945

Keep Me Humble Lord, 1947

Look For Me For I'll Be There, 1948

Meet Me Where There'll Be No More Good Bye, 1945

Not A Word, 1947

Oh Yes He Will, 1951

Oh Yes He's Mine, 1944

Roll Memory's Roll

Smile When Things Go Wrong, 1945

Sometimes My Load's So Hard To Bear, 1949

Songs Of Praise, 1951

Paste, Charles H. (continued)

When You've Done Your Best, 1953

Stay Thou Near Lord, 1948

This Little Light Of Mine I'm Going To Let It Shine,
     (Paste arranged but selected by L. Bowles)

There'll Be Joy Up There, 1946

There's A Bright Light Shining On My Soul, 1947

There's A Change In Me, 1944

Tis Morning Dawn A Brighter Day, 1949

When I Behold My Saviors Face, 1944

When I Get Home, 1947

I'm Going To Reap Just What You Sow - You Going To Reap
     Just What You Sow, 1948

You'll Find Him There, 1948

Parker, Ada

Holy God, Ada Parker Publ., Louisville, Ky., 1963

I'm Thirsty Give Me Water, 1961

Oh What A Wonderful Jesus, 1961

Parker, Edward N.

Father Alone, pbc 2023 Piru St., Compton, Calif., (new
     arrangement)

Lord Revive Us

Parker, Marylou Coleman

Just Keep On, pbc Parker's Music Studio, Mt. Vernon, Ill.,
     1949

Lord Have Mercy, pbc, 1949

Please Dear Lord, 1948

When Jesus Comes, 1950

Parker, Marylou Coleman (continued)

   Why Can't You Believe, 1949, (Ded: Birmingham Blue Jay
      Singers)

   Yes He'll Be There, 1948

   Yes I Know, 1949

Pearson, Dorothy Pasco

   My Saviour And Kin, RM, pbc, 1950

Pennington, Arlena

   Jesus Filled Me, 1961

   In My God's Way, 1961, (Copy secured from owner
      Pennington, 1110 W. 64th St., Chicago, Ill.)

Penny, Carolyn

   The Lord Will Lift You, Hicks Music Studio, 9922 Ostend
      Ave., Cleveland, Ohio, (Ded: Hartford Youth and Young
      Adult Dept. Hartford, Conn.)

Pettis, Tessie Mae

   I Want To See Jesus Don't You, pbc Chicago, Ill., 1948

   I'm Going To Take A Stand For Jesus, 1948

   There's No Friend Like Jesus, VD, 1948

   I Want To Be In That Number, LB, 1945

Pointer, Rev. A.H.

   There is Something That Makes Me Know I His Child, LB,
      1945

Posey, Edward Sr.

   I'll Get Along Somehow, pbc Chicago, Ill., 1946

   I'm Going To Make It In, 1946

   I'm Sometimes Weeping, 1946

   Jesus Is Looking For Me, 1946

Posey, Edward Sr. (continued)

   Lord If I Try, 1946

   He Will Roll The Stone Away, 1950

Powell, J.P.

   God's Going To Pour Out His Raft, Powell's Gospel Recording
      Home Studio, Chicago, Ill., 1945

   He Abides In My Soul, LB, 1945

   His Spirit Moves In Me, First Church of Deliverance, (Ded:
      Choir of the South Side)

   Holy Is The Lord, 1956, (Feat: Versatile Dukes of Harmony)

   In A Moment A Twinkling Of An Eye, RM, 1945

   The Lord Is My Shepard, LB, 1944

Powell, Virginia Hadassah

   Let Jesus Rule, L. Parker Music Studio, Phila., Pa., 1946

   Tis Jesus, 1944

Price, Charles A.

   I'm On My Way To Heaven Everyday, pbc, 1961

Pringle, Clarence E.

   Have Faith In God, Pringle's Music Center, Grace Bonner
      Music Studio, Cincinnati, Ohio, 1964

   I Want Jesus To Walk With Me

   I Will Trust In The Lord

Pringle, Charles E.

   Lean On Me, (Feat: Fairbanks Twins)

   On The Other Side, 1959

Prichard, Mabell

   I Know I Trust In Jesus, LB, 1945

Proctor, Carrie D. Cowin

    Light And Darkness Don't Mix, Miller's Music Studio, Gary
        Ind., 1955

Prior, Mason

    I Love To Tell The Old Old Story, pbc, 1946

    I Pray I Pray Jesus I Pray, pbc, 1946

Prior, R.L.

    Jesus Want's To Live In The Heart Of Man, LB, 1945

Quillian, Rufus L.

    I'll Go With My Saviour All The Way, TF, 1946

Radford, Emmery

    What A Companion, Father Anderson, GS, 1948

Ramey, Verlie

    One Of These Mornings, pbc, Chicago, Ill., 1957

    Somewhere In God's Kingdom, 1957

Rasberry, Raymond

    Deliverance Will Come, pbc, Cleveland, Ohio, 1961

    Every Round Of The Ladder Brings Me Closer, 1959

    I Want To Be More Like Jesus, 1953, (Sung: Ward Singers,
        Henrietta Wady, Sally Smith Singers)

    I'll Let Nothing Separate Me, MM, 1955

    Jesus Is All To Me, 1956

    Jesus The King Of Kings, 1959

    Lord In The New Jerusalem, 1960

    Oh What You Do For Christ Will Last, 1963

    We're Crossing Over, 1958

Ray, Minnie

    If You Just Wait, pbc St. Louis, Mo., 1955

    Lord Have I Failed, 1955

Rector, Walter

    Lead The Way, MM, 1949

    Moments of Prayer, 1949

    The Twenty-Third Psalm, 1951

    Yes I Know, 1951

Reed, Barbara

    He's Calling Today (Jesus Is Tenderly Calling), John
        Watley, 1957, (Sung: Barbara Reed and Reed Specials)

    Hold Out To The End, MM, 1957

Reed, Clarence

    Christ Died For Us On Calvery, 1964

    Hands Of My Dear God, pbc 1340 N. Larabee St., Chicago
        Ill., 1963

    I'm Working While It's Day, 1964

    Marching In The House Of Prayer, 1962

    She Cast Her All, 1963

    You Can Make It With The Help Of God, 1963

Reed, Yolanda Smiley

    Thank You Lord For Taking Me Through, Miller's Music
        Studio, Gary, Ind., 1946

Reese, Terry J.

    Lord I Wonder If I'm Right Or Wrong, pbc South Birmingham,
        Ala., Jackson Music Co., Birmingham, Ala., 1945

Reese, L.J., Jr.

    Sword And Shield, 1960, (Sung: Corinthian Gospel Singers)

    By Playing My Music

Reeves, Walter L.

    Be Ready Judgement Day, pbc, N.Y., 1947

Rice, Harry Wilhoite

    Do You Realize, pbc Jamaica, N.Y., 1945

    It's All Right Now, 1946

    It's So Good To Walk With Jesus, 1946

    Jesus Hears My Prayers, 1952

    Jesus Will Take Me Through, 1952

    Keep The Trust, 1952

    Lord Only You, 1946

    My Prayer

    Now's The Time To Come To Jesus

    Someone (Needs Jesus Today)

    Talk It Over With The Lord

    There's No Other Friend Like Jesus

    Want To Know Jesus Is Taking Care Of Me

    When I Go To God In Prayer

Richardson, Anne Bell

    Come To The Fountain Of Life, pbc Chicago, Ill., 1949

    He's My Saviour, pbc, 1952

    I Am Satisfied With Jesus, pbc, 1949

    In The Shelter Of The Rock, Let Me Hide, pbc, 1948

    There Are So Many Sorrows, pbc, 1952

Robinson, Cora F.D.

    Jesus Is The Truest Friend, pbc, 1961

Robinson, Edward G.

    I Saw The Beautiful Light, RM, 1956

    I Want To Be Ready, 1957

    Sign Of The Judgement, 1962, (Pianist for Mahalia Jackson.
        This is a hand written pencil score.)

    What A Wonderful Saviour, 1959

    When I See Jesus, 1957

Robinson, Helen

    Be Still And Know, R.R. Publ. Co., Chicago, Ill., 1955

    Jesus Lives In Me, MM, 1961

    Straighten Out Your Life, 1966

Robinson, Jessie Mae

    When I Say My Prayer, 1955

Robinson, Joe L.

    He's Watching Over Me, pbc, 1960, (Sung: Virginia Davis,
        Marshall and Robisonians of Chicago, Ill.)

    I Shall Live Eternally, Jolero Music Studio, Chicago, Ill.,
        1961

    I'm Going To Keep On, Jolero, 1961

Robinson, Josephus

    Don't You Let Nobody Turn You Around And Swing Low,
        Singtime Publ. Co., Chicago, Ill., 1952

    (Arrangements of)

    Let Us Break Bread Together

    Little David Play On Your Harp

    Sing A Song For Jesus Every Day And He'll Answer

Robinson, Josephus (continued)

    We Shall Walk Through The Valley

    Let Us Look Ever Look To Jesus

Rogers, Warren

    I Will Mind God, pbc Detroit, Mich., 1947

    Others, 1965

Roots, Jane

    Trouble Is Mine, 1956, (Sung: Pilgrim Travelers)

Ross, L. Nathan C.

    Father Lead Me, pbc Chicago, Ill., 1963

    He Is All My Joy, 1964

Ross, Johnnie

    Touch, Touch Me, MM, 1955

Roundtree, Delores

    Only God Can Know, LB, 1966

Royal, Thelma

    Take Jesus Wherever You Go, pbc Cleveland, Ohio, 1953

Royster, Charles

    Call On Jesus' Secret Prayer, Brown's Music House,
        Indianapolis, Ind., 1950

Rubin, Mary G.

    Don't You Know God Has Done Enough For Me, pbc Calif., 1948

    He Stopped Me From Straying One Day, 1949

    His Name Is Everything To Me, 1962, (Feat: Stars of Harmony)

    I Have A Radio Television In My Heart, 1949

Rubin, Mary G. (continued)

    I'll Be There, Right There, Won't You, 1952

    I've Tried To Count My Every Blessing, 1962

    Jesus Lead Me All The Way, 1948

    There's A Mansion Waiting For Me, 1949

Russell, Virginia

    By And By, pbc, 1949

    Jesus You Know, 1948

    When Jesus Comes, 1948

Ryan, William H.

    Jesus Is Precious To My Soul, Ryan and Dickons, Chicago,
        Ill., 1962

Scott, Benjamin (The following entires published by the
                   composer, Chicago, Ill.)

    Are You Satisfied, 1964

    Have You Invested In The Heavenly Kingdom I Have, 1964

    Hard To Find Another Man Like Jesus, 1963

    He Is Everywhere You May Go, 1965

    I Just Can't Make It By Myself Alone, 1963

    I'm Learning, 1963

    It's Only God Who Knows The Heart, 1963

    With Christ We Shall Reign Forever To Be, 1963

    Glorious Day (When It Comes), 1963

Seay, Beatrice

    Jesus Is The Best Friend Of All, pbc Cleveland, Ohio, 1948

    I Want To Know More About Jesus, MM, 1967 (Sung: Coralee
        Gospel Singers)

    Oh Lord Send The Light, 1957

Seay, Beatrice (continued)

    Some Day I'll Get My Crown, 1957

    Wait Until He Comes, 1958

Shropshire, Louise

    His Precious Blood, pbc Cincinnati, Ohio, 1954

    Crucified For Me

    I Know Jesus Pilots Me

    Are You Worthy To Take Communion

    I'm A Child Of Christ, The King

    I'm Longing To Go There Someday

    If My Jesus Will

    I'm Trying My Best To Get Home To See Jesus

Silvester, Norman

    Take God Along With You, MM, 1954

Simmons, Leo

    The Golden Stairs, MM, 1954

Simmons, Rosa L.

    He's A Wonder In My Soul, 1946

Simmons, Sara

    God Means Everything, RM, 1960

Sims, Martina

    I Want To See Jesus For Myself, Studio of Sacred Publ.,
       Baltimore, Md., 1946

Smallwood, Ann

    In My Father's House, Savoy, 1958

Smallwood, Ann (continued)

    Reach Out And Touch Him, Savoy, 1958, (Sung: Imperial
        Gospel Singers)

    There's Nothing Too Right For God, Savoy, 1960

Smallwood, Eugene D.

    Let's Go Back To Our Father's Praying Ground, 1943

    When He Spoke, TF, 1951

Smallwood, Rev. E.D.

    Without Jesus Nothing At All, 1961

Smith, A.A.

    God Can't Fail, Savoy, 1960, (Sung: Prof. Charles Taylor)

    I Heard The News, Savoy, 1960, (Rec: North Philadelphia
        Jrs.)

Smith, Bertha W.

    Just Keep Still, words and music Willa Mae Ford, 1938

Smith, Bessie L.

    Around The Throne After While, 1947

    I Know I'm Saved Unto Thee

Smith, Dora Helm

    Thy Will Be Done, Rev. Walter Lewis Gospel Music Studio,
        L.A., Calif., 1955

Smith, Geneser

    Father Thy Will Be Done, 1966

    God Is A Wonder

    The Half Has Not Been Told

    He's Sweeter As The Days Roll By

Smith, Geneser (continued)

   The Holy Ghost That Jesus Is Giving Away, (Sung: Smith
       Singers)

   I'm Not Worthy

   The Chapel

   Oh What A Day, 1955

   Rely On Me, 1955

Smith, Harold

   Don't Limit God, MM, 1959, (Ded: First Church Of Deliver-
       ance Radio Choir)

   I Know There's Rest, (Feat: Radio Choir of Rev. Charles
       Franklin, Detroit, Mich.)

   I'll Never Forget That Day, FCD, 1956

   I'm Depending On The Lord, MM, 1959

   I've Been Redeemed, MM, 1959, (Sung: First Church Deliver-
       ance Radio Choir)

   King Jesus Is Calling You, MM, 1959

   How Wonderful It Is, MM, 1961

   Faith In Jesus, Rev. C.L. Franklin's Church, 1961

   What Shall I Render Unto God, 1967

Smith, Louis Frances

   The Land Of Rest, pbc Santa Monica, Calif., 1949

   Who Can Stand At The Judgement Day

Smith, Ophillia C.

   Salvation Is Free, pbc, 1949

Smith, Richard Allen

   God Is Our Father, pbc, 1948

Smith, Willa Mae Ford

   My Mind's Made Up And My Heart Is Fixed, LB, 1939

Spain, Olivia

   In A Few More Days, MM, 1954, (Sung: Alex Bradford)

Spencer, Lucille

   I'm Going There And See, pbc Cleveland, Ohio, 1946

Stennett, Samuel

   On Jordan's Stormy Banks I Stand, MM, 1952, (Sung:
     Simon and Acker Singers, L.A., Calif.)

Stewart, Evan

   Did Jesus Die In Vain, pbc Winnemac, Ind., 1953, (Distrib-
     uted by White's Beauty Shop, Chicago, Ill.)

Stanley, Francis T.

   I'll Take Jesus As My Friend, pbc Baltimore, Md., 1957

Strawther, Rev. Joe

   He Is A Friend To Me, LB, 1960

   Pilot Me, orig. words of Wm. Washington, Coleman's Church
     Supply, Cleveland, Ohio, pbc, 1960

Taliafero, Delores E.

   He Made It Right, RM, RM, 1952, (Sung: Meditation Singers
     New Liberty Baptist Church, Detroit, Mich.)

   What Do You Need, 1952

Tall, Jeanette Jackson

   He Blesses Me, Robert J. Holly, 1946, (Ded: Steadman
     Sisters)

Taylor, Alex

    Walking The Streets Of Gold, pbc, 1954, (Copies from composer, 159 W. Main, Peru, Ind.)

Taylor, Prof. Charles Dewitt

    The Bells, Craft Music Publ., N.Y., 1955

    The Blood of Jesus, Charles Taylor, Savoy, 1960

    God's Got A Television, Craft, 1955

    I Must Live Until Morning, Savoy, 1958

    I'll See It Through, Savoy, 1958

    I'll Tell The World, Craft, 1956

    The Message (Look Up And Live), Playmar, 1959

    Religion Like It Used To Be, Craft, 1955

    Six Months, Savoy, 1959

Taylor, Hattie May

    I've Got A Building Built On High, MM, 1944

    When He Looks On The Lamb's Book In Glory, pbc Washington, D.C., 1945

Taylor, Raphael

    Welcome Home, Ve, 1951, (Rec: Pilgrim Travelers)

Taylor, Roumel William

    I'm So Glad He's Mine, MM, pbc Phila. Pa., 1945

    Oh Praise The Lord, MM, 1945

    Since I Gave My Heart To The Lord, pbc, 1947

    This Same Jesus Cares For You And Me, 1946

Teasley, Josephine

    My Help Cometh From The Lord, pbc St. Louis, Mo., 1962, (Sung: Teasley Singers)

Teasley, Josephine (continued)

   Prayer Keeps Me Marching On, 1965

Teverbaugh, Faygon Jr.

   My Blessed Home Above, MM, 1946

Tharp, Rosetta

   Can't Do Wrong And Get By, Cyprus Music Co., N.Y., 1956

   So High So Low, 1956

   Up Above My Head I Hear Music In The Air, American Acad-
      emy of Music, N.Y., 1949

Thatcher, Enik Mark

   A Highway To Heaven Is The One For Me, Gospel Songs,
      Detroit, Mich., 1956

   I'll Walk Arm and Arm With Jesus, 1956

   Jesus Is The Same Today, 1950

   Then Jesus Will Dry Away Your Tears

   The World Doesn't Have A Single Thing To Me

Thomas, Alvetta

   What Prayer Will Do For You, pbc 4844 N. Glen Ave., St.
      Louis, Mo., 1961

Thomas, Arlington H.

   He'll Always Answer Prayer, TF, VD, LB, 1953, (Ded: to
      his friends)

Thomas, John

   Dear Lord I Pray, LB, 1953

   Down To The River, LB, 1953

   He's All Right With Me, LB, 1953

   He's A Light Of My Heart, LB, 1953

Thomas, John (continued)

    I'll Follow You Jesus All The Way, LB, 1953

    I'm Coming Home Someday, LB, 1953

    Lord I Want To Go Home, 1954

    My Home, 1954

    There's Coming A Sweeter Day, 1954

    We've Got To Move Someday

Thompson, Will

    Jesus Is All The World To Me, VD, LB, 1904, (1904 renewal
      by Pope Publ. Co.)

Thorton, Armenta DeMoss

    Grace, Joy, Peace and Happiness, Wilson, L.A., Calif.

    Jesus Requires Of You To Be Ture, 1947

Tindley, C.A.

    We'll Understand Better By And By, MM, 1951

    Live It There, C.A. Tinley Jr., Hill and Dale, 1952

Turner, Kyle

    Take My Mother's Hand, Ve, 1954, (Pilgrim Travelers)

    Worried Traveler, Ve, 1954

    Who Am I

Twigg, Atron Jamison

    He Knows My Name, Twigg Music Studio, Memphis, Tenn., 1951

Tyler, Elder E.

    Jesus Will Never Let You Down, An, 1947

Ufford, Rev. E.S.

    Throw Out The Life Line, MM, 1951, (Sung: Sally Martin
       Singers)

Vance, Agusta

    I Just Can't Keep It To Myself Alone, MM, 1942

Veasey, Lyza

    I'm Trusting In His Word, pbc, Chicago, Ill., 1958

Walker, Albertina

    Comfort Me, MM, 1960, (Sung: Caravans)

    Jesus Heard My Earnest Plea, MM, 1955, (Rec: Caravans)

    Jesus Won't Deny Me (He Won't Deny Me), MM, 1957

    Lord I Want To Thank You, MM, 1955

Wallace, Marvenia

    Wasn't That One Happy Day When Jesus Washed My Sins Away,
       pbc Hagerstown, Md., 1945

Wallace, Rosey J.

    Can't Turn Around Now, MM, 1962, (Sung and Rec: Christian
       Tabernacle Choir, Phila., Pa. Gospel Recording
       LP 1365)

    Just To God Be True, MM, 1962

Wallace, Sylvester Sr.

    My God, pbc Chicago, Ill., 1953

Ward, Clara

    God Is God, Playmar, 1960

    Great Is The Lord, Carol Ward, 1956

    He's Watching Over You, Savoy, 1959

    How I Got Over, An, 1954, (Rec: on Garthon Records 674)

Ward, Clara (continued)

    I Feel The Holy Spirit, Wards House of Music, Phila., Pa.,
        1954

    I Just Can't Make It By Myself, Ben L. Speer Music Publ.,
        Nashville, Tenn., 1958

    I Know It Was The Lord, 1953

    In His Arms, 1958

    I'll Anchor In The Harbor Of The Lord, 1953

    I'm Going Home, 1955

    King Jesus Is All I Need, 1953

    Oh Gabriel, words and music Rev. W. Herbert Brewster and
        C. Ward, 1955

    Our God Is Real, 1958

    Trying To Get Home, (Rec: C.L. Franklin and Franklin
        Singers)

    We're Going To Have A Time, Savoy, 1959

Washington, Martha

    No Greater Love Than This, LB, 1962

    Tell Jesus For I Know He'll Give Relief, MM, 1955

Waters, Ethel E.

    There Is Nothing My God Cannot Do, Watercrest Prod., St.
        Louis, Mo., 1966

    With The Help Of The Lord I Will Overcome, C.A.D. Gift
        Shop Printing, St. Louis, Mo., 1965

Waters, Mary L.

    I'm Living To Live Again, Waters House of Sacred Music,
        Springfield, Ill., 1963

Watford, Paul

    Religion In The Home, 1955

Watrous, Rosalee Dillard

    I'll Be Satisfied, 1947, (Sung: Watrous, Dewittee Singers,
       Ruth Davis Pianist)

Webb, George W.

    Stand Up For Jesus, LB, 1951, (Ded: Willa Mae Ford Smith
       and the W.M.F. Smith Specials)

Webb, Willia Jaiah

    Christian Duty, Mahalia Jackson Music Inc., Soul Selling
       Agent, HR, MJ, 1959

    Jesus Is The Answer He's All I Need, RM, 1957

    I Want To Know If He Will Welcome Me There, RM, 1954

    Lord Keep Me, 1959

    Will You Be There, 1958

Webber, Sylvia J.W.

    When God Plants His Foot Steps, pbc, 1964

Webster, William M.

    Lord How Long Will We Have To Wait, J.P. Powell, Jr.,
       Chicago, Ill., 1944

West, Naomi

    He's So Wonderful In His Love, pbc, Chicago, Ill., 1961

Weston, Dave

    The Great Invitation, First Church of Deliverance, 1955

    He's Coming For His Church, MM, 1958

    I Have A New Outlook On Life, MM, 1963

    Jesus Knows How It Feels Not To Be Loved, MM, 1963

    The Time To Shout, 1956

White, Herbert

    Jesus Is All And All, RM, 1952

Widham, Aaron

    Peace Peace In Jesus, Widham Studio, St. Louis, Mo., 1954

    There's Rest For The Weary, 1947

    You Got The River Of Jordan Across, 1941, (Feat: V. Davis)

Widham, Cornelius

    Jesus Will Make A Way For You, MM, 1952

Widman, Violet

    I Will Have A Happy Time, Colemans, Cleveland, Ohio, 1958

    Feel Like Traveling On, 1960

Wiley, Mary

    Call Up Heaven, Blairs Music Publ., Detroit, Mich., 1961

Wikerson, Walter

    There's Nothing Can Keep Me From Serving The Lord, Lula
       Raybond, Toledo, Ohio, MM, 1942

Williams, Dimetrus

    So Glad I've Been Lifted, MM, 1957, (Sung: Gospel Cavaleers)

Williams, Eddy

    Carry Me Back, RM, 1965

    The Debt I Owe To The Lord (The Blood of Jesus), MM, 1961

    God's Unchanging Hand, 1961, (Sung: Caravans)

    If You Want To See Jesus, 1958, (Sung: Caravans)

    I'll Tear The Wall Down, MM, 1960, (Sung: Crusaders)

    I'm A Child Of The King, RM, 1965

Williams, Eddy (continued)

   I'm Glad I Counted The Cost, MM, 1960

   Lord Keep Me Day By Day, MM, 1959, (Sung: Eddie Williams,
      and Caravans)

   There Must Be A God Somewhere, RM, 1965

Williams, Lucille

   God Has Everything You Need, LB, 1965

Williams, Lucy E. Campbell

   Come, Lord, Jesus Abide With Me, 1963

Williams, Marian

   I Shall Wear A Crown, 1959, (Sung: Stars of Faith)

Williams, Mory M.

   I'm Going To Hold On Until The End, Mary E. Lacy Moore,
      pbc, 1957

   Lord I Cannot Make The Journey All By Myself, 1957

Williams, Omega

   Give Me Grace, RM, 1958

Williams, Willie May

   Can't Make This Journey By Myself, 1962

   Jesus, He Is The Only One, 1958

Willis, Floriene Watson

   Lord I'll Go, 1958

Wilmac, Effie

   I Said Oh No I Just Can't Stop Now, pbc, Chicago., Ill., 1965

   Just To Weep, 1963

   Time Winding Up, 1963

Index to the Bibliography

The numbers in this index are entry numbers.

Index to the Catalogue

The numbers in this index are page numbers.

ABOUT THE COMPILER

Irene V. Jackson, formerly Assistant Professor of Ethnomusicology at Yale University, has published in such journals as *Black Perspectives in Music, Sing-Out,* and *Freeing the Spirit.* She is currently ethnomusicologist-in-residence at Howard University and general editor of the Afro-American Hymnal Project of the Commission for Black Ministries of the National Episcopal Church.

Afro-American Religious Music: A Bibliography and a Catalogue of Gospel Music. Compiled by Irene V. Jackson. Westport, Connecticut: Greenwood Press, 1979. xiv + 210 pp. Index. Hard cover, $19.95. This bibliography provides references to many little-known sources for the study of black religious music. The first section categorizes citations under such headings as ethnomusicology, dance, folklore, religious folksongs, black religion, Caribbean culture, and Afro-American history, culture, anthropology, and sociology. All sources are indexed and cross-referenced. The second section, a catalog of published gospel music copyrighted between 1937 and 1965, lists the composer, arranger, title, publishing company, and copyright year. A chapter immediately preceding this section describes how to distinguish between white and black gospel music styles.